Remember to Live!

Embracing the Second Half of Life

THOMAS RYAN

PAULIST PRESS
New York / Mahwah, NJ

Cover images: Courtesy of Shutterstock.com.
Cover and book design by Lynn Else

Library of Congress Cataloging-in-Publication Data

Ryan, Thomas, Father.
    Remember to live! : embracing the second half of life / Thomas Ryan.
      p. cm.
    Includes bibliographical references (p.   ).
    ISBN 978-0-8091-4758-8 (alk. paper) — ISBN 978-1-61643-134-1 1. Older Christians—Religious life. 2. Aging—Religious aspects—Christianity. 3. Death—Religious aspects—Christianity. 4. Life—Religious aspects—Christianity. I. Title.
    BV4580.R93 2011
    248.8'5—dc23

                                    2011040211

Published by Paulist Press
997 Macarthur Boulevard
Mahwah, New Jersey 07430

www.paulistpress.com

Printed and bound in the
United States of America

To my father and mother,
Francis and Genevieve,
who were wonderful models for us
in both their living and their dying

Contents

Acknowledgments

Every project of this nature involves the appreciated contributions of many people along the way. I am grateful to Maurice Gardiol, Cosette Odier, and Josette Morel for providing the impetus to make the reflections on these themes available in print and for their enrichment of them.

A heartfelt thanks as well is extended to all those who have shared something of their own story in these pages: Karen Nedzela, Beth O'Mara, Susan Barylo, Kevin Ryan, Gwendolyn Gresham, Maria Teresa Porcile, Sister Fleurette Sweeney, SC, Pauline Schmelz, Mary Claire Ryan, Jackie and Dave McMakin and Michael Ryan.

I want to express my deep appreciation to Sister Pauline Fritz, SSND, for graciously contributing the valuable Appendix resource, "Peace through Planning."

Thanks, too, to Brother Dominic Smith, FSC, for providing a quiet and convenient place to work when it was needed at certain stages of the writing.

And a special thanks to my editor Jim Quigley, to senior copy editor Susan Heyboer O'Keefe, and to managing editor Donna Crilly, all of whom made appreciable contributions to the publication of this book.

Introduction

When I turned fifty, I didn't want to have just the conventional dinner party and birthday cake. I wanted to do something more substantial and meaningful to me personally. And as I was at the time the director of a center for spirituality that not only offered programs but provided lodging for participants, I was in a position to do it.

My birthday fell on a weekend, so I decided to lead a weekend retreat on the theme of "Savoring Life by Facing Our Mortality." My siblings, a number of friends, and others who were simply intrigued by the theme composed the group of participants. We engaged with some of the topics that comprise the chapters of this book, entering into periods of quiet reflection after a presentation, doing some journaling, then sharing the fruit of our inner work with one another in small groups. And in the middle of it, on Saturday evening, we balanced the seriousness with the fun and laughter and camaraderie of a party celebrating life.

At the end, people expressed deep appreciation for the opportunity to engage in the process of facing their mortality squarely and with eyes wide open. Even within the short span of a weekend, it was clear to us that doing so made us much clearer minded about a few things.

First, that there is very little in our culture that supports our doing this. The advertisements we see on the TV screen and in our magazines and newspapers would have us believe that if we get enough sleep, take the right vitamins, and exercise regularly, we will live indefinitely.

Second, that when we do face the fact that this precious gift of life on planet Earth is not given in limitless supply, it clarifies our vision and intention about the use of the time we have.

We stop taking things for granted and putting things off for "someday."

Third, that while engaging with some of the topics involved may have seemed a bit morbid at the outset, we quickly experienced that doing so took us in the direction of more conscious living and thus toward fuller life. It helped us sort out our priorities and realign the use of our time and energy and material resources to keep first things first.

My own reflection in the aftermath of the weekend was that this process was too valuable to do just once. Given the strength of our resistance to facing our mortality, it would be helpful to engage in it repeatedly, to keep chipping away at that resistance, allowing ourselves to become freer within and face the future, not with fear, but with thanksgiving both for the time that has been given and for the time that continues to be given now.

So I committed myself to offering this retreat somewhere at least once a year as a way of continuing to do my own inner work and of inviting others to do the same. After the second or third time around, it became clear to me that more time would enable people to go deeper with more lasting effect in their living. So I added a full day to the weekend model for those who couldn't afford to take a full week for it, and expanded it to a weeklong process for those who could.

One of the groups that entered into this experience was an association of Protestant clergy in Geneva, Switzerland. After the retreat, a few of them approached me to say how much they would like to bring this to people in their congregations, and asked whether I would be open to sharing my material with them toward that end. "Why not?" I thought. "The more people we can reach, the better!" And so we began to work together on organizing the material, enriching it with resources from their own personal and pastoral experience and cultural context, and publishing it in book form in French.[1]

That pushed me to begin working on something similar in English. So over the next two to three years, I began devoting available time to writing an expanded version, the result of which you are holding in your hands. The stories and witnessing contained in these pages represent the harvest of working these themes with people over the last fifteen years, as well as my own increased sensitivity to the richness and complexity of the questions involved.

The themes are of universal application. None of us can escape the realities of aging, illness, loss, and death. The question is: How will we engage with these realities—with fear and trepidation, or with a desire to learn the lessons they have to teach and to thus grow through our encounter with them? As indicated by the title of this book, engaging with these themes is an invitation to fuller and deeper *living*. The evangelist John writes that Christ came that we might have life and have it abundantly (John 10:10), so let us open our minds and hearts in confidence to the unique contribution that each of life's seasons makes toward that abundant living.

This book can also be used as a resource in educational programs and for personal growth-and-development support groups. The first six chapters are pertinent to all. The seventh, "Your Life Now," is aimed particularly at those in the mid-forties-to-retirement range of their lives. The last chapter, "Remember to Live!" while addressed to us all, has those in their retirement years specially in mind.

Individual readers are encouraged to make of this a kind of workbook to be picked up and reviewed whenever one theme or another becomes pertinent in their lived experience with the passing of the years. Revisiting the topics opened up in these pages time and again expands our zone of acceptance and renews our intention to respond positively and constructively to the grace hidden in the experiences of each. Whenever I lead a retreat on these subjects, I myself am the first beneficiary.

Much of my ministry has been devoted to the work for Christian unity. This work goes forward on the intellectual plane, such as theological dialogue, and on the applied level in the social sphere, such as work for justice and care of the environment. In the realm that has come to be known as spiritual ecumenism, this work for unity among the followers of Jesus also takes the form of retreats and cosponsored congregational renewal events that bring together members of different Christian traditions for worship, community, and mission.[2] All are necessary, but in this season of my ministry, I have a clear preference for the approach of spiritual ecumenism. I want to give my time and energy to methods and means that reach the people in our congregations and that hold the possibility of changing their angle on living in a positive direction.

These themes can certainly be worked with by members of the same tradition in a group setting, but when they are engaged in by people of different denominations, they have an additional benefit: they make us aware of how much we share, of how all that we hold in common in Christ is so much broader and deeper than anything that still divides us.

And when we marshal the resources of our faith to face the challenging realities of life together, we grow in fellowship and love for one another. We meet one another on a deeply human level. We grow in our awareness of each other's faith and fervor. We share the gifts of ritual, prayer, and pastoral practice from our traditions. And because of the relationships created, we will be there for each other in the challenges of the midlife years as well as in the retirement years—befriending, accompanying, supporting in good times and in bad, in sickness and in health. We will join hands with one another and pool our resources in addressing the needs we see around us, and in so doing we will be good news for the communities in which we live. We will, in short, be walking the path that leads to Life together, providing inspiration for others as well as comfort and challenge to one another all along the way. And isn't that what life in the community of the Church is all about?

Long Pond

A protected bay
where once fishermen
dropped their hooks
becomes cut off from the sea
by offshore winds
and blowing sand.
A ridge of dunes now
stands between the two.

Years pass, and Long Pond's
salty water turns to fresh.
Reeds and cat-tails
take root and grow,
now converging from all sides
and foreshadowing the day
when marshland thickens
and wet meadow turns to forest.

In a conspiracy against permanence,
waves will scrape more grains of sand
from the hard-packed ocean floor
and hurl them up onto the beach
where sun will dry them out
and wind will sweep them
into the forest where they will choke
the roots and kill the trees
and turn it into desert.

Who will believe then
that one day fishermen
let out the coil of their anchor here

and brought up living things
from the sea? But as I stand astride
two eras I can see that it was so
and will thus come to be, and more—
the ziggybugs are now writing it
on the water of Long Pond just below:
nothing holds its place, including me.

Chapter One

Aging

Aging is not enough in itself. Aging well is the real goal of life. To allow ourselves to age without vitality, without purpose, without growth is simply to get old rather than to age well as we go. We must be a gift to the world someway, somehow, for someone.

—Joan Chittister

I was sitting in an airport waiting lounge and, across from me, a woman was reading one of the country's popular weekly news-magazines. The words emblazoned on the cover caught my eye: "Live without Aging: It's Coming Soon!"

The story inside reported on the proceedings of a conference organized by the Massachusetts Institute of Technology on the future of such health technologies as stem-cell research, pharmacogenomology, genetic therapy, nanotechnology, resveratrol (the famous substance with antioxydizing powers contained in red wine), prostheses, and implants.[1] Several bio-gerontologists (one of them the author of a book entitled *Ending Aging*) were quoted at length to the effect that it will soon be possible to counter the devastating effects of the passing of time.

A research scientist among the presenters said he was convinced that the breakthroughs of science, notably in the field of molecular biology, would soon put an end to the causes of aging. He expressed confidence that before the end of the century we would be able to greatly reduce the number of deaths due to aging.

Another speaker said that we must "wake up to the fact that aging kills." One hundred thousand people on the planet die every day of old age, he reported, then insisting: "We must put an end to this horror film, to this human catastrophe." He compared the aging of the human body to that of a house. If one conscientiously looks after its upkeep, a residence can traverse epochs. In the same way, the human body can aspire to immortality—on the condition that we repair the molecular and cellular damage caused by aging.

In other words, aging is no longer an insoluble problem, just an engineering challenge.

To be sure, every civilization has tried in its own way to slow down the aging process. Druids and European alchemists, Chinese sages and Indian medicine men, have consecrated their lives to finding the famous fountain of youth or to concocting a secret elixir for long life. Could one of the contributing factors to the reemergence in our time of an "immortalist movement" be that millions of baby boomers are now in their sixties?

One of the conference's futurologists—himself sixty, and recognizing that the technologies being spoken of would not be accessible yet for some years—acknowledged that he followed a rigorous fitness program as well as a special diet, in addition to taking 250 pills, vitamins, and vitamin supplements a day, along with ten glasses of alkaline water and ten cups of green tea. His aim, he said, was to minimalize the aging process while waiting for the "great day" when science will permit us to "reprogram" our bodies, "placing our destiny in our own hands."

Several other methods for delaying the aging process were featured in the newsmagazine article: exercising regularly, eating better and eating less, making love more often, taking vitamin D supplements, getting enough sleep, maintaining muscle mass with weight workouts, stimulating the brain with complex mental activities, and maintaining good dental hygiene.

No one would quarrel with attempts to help people live longer in good health and with mobility. At the same time, one could observe that many contemporary sociocultural phenomena—death cults such as abortion, euthanasia, teen suicide, and violent entertainment—are essentially attempts to facilitate an illusion of control over human destiny. One of the objectives of this book is to help us embrace aging gracefully as a fact of life.

The Quest for Immortality

Just before the onset of his final illness, the spiritual teacher and writer Eknath Easwaren, reflecting on the efforts of science and biology to discover ways of continuously regenerating all body tissues toward a vision of human immortality, asked what might be *lost* by focusing so relentlessly on retaining physical youth at all costs. He then recounted a story from one of Hinduism's great epics, the *Mahabharata*, about Yayati, a king who wanted to remain forever young.

In the story, as King Yayati sees his strength and vigor slipping away, he can't help noticing that his five sons, in the full flush of their youth, are able to enjoy the entire range of physical pleasures. So he calls in his oldest son and says to him:

> "Because of your love for me, I have a great boon to ask. Won't you exchange your youth for my age? I am still so hungry for all the pleasures of the flesh, and my youth is flying away from me." Not surprisingly, the first son refuses his father's bizarre request.
>
> Then the king calls in his second son, who pleads, "Ask me anything else." The third son in his turn and then the fourth say, "No, Father, that's not something I can give."
>
> Finally he comes to his fifth son, Puru, saying, "Your brothers have all declined my request. I can understand that they would not want to give up their youth, but my desire is so great and my thirst for these pleasures is unquenchable. Will you, out of your love for me, consider letting me be young again?"
>
> Puru, with wisdom well beyond his years and deep spiritual insight, quietly replies, "Is that all, Father? I thought you were going to ask for something really

serious. If it is only my physical vigor and my capacity to enjoy sensory pleasures that you want, I give them to you without regrets."

The exchange takes place. As Puru becomes old, King Yayati becomes young again. His hair turns black, his eyes brighten, his muscles regain their strength, and he feels the passionate energies of youth welling up in his heart. His son tells him, "Father, please go and have all the pleasures you want. I will be seated here meditating and repeating my mantra, thinking about the joy of the Lord, which is not of this body."

King Yayati paints all the ancient cities of north India red with his revels. Round and round he goes through the whole smorgasbord of pleasures until finally, alienated and disillusioned, he begins to wonder why the fulfillment he is seeking seems further away than ever. After some years, he comes back completely ashamed and asks his son to forgive him.

"You are not my son," he tells Puru. "You are my teacher. There is no end to these pleasures, and the more I pursue them, the less I enjoy them."

And the son says, "No, no, Father. It is not I who has taught you. You discovered for yourself what following the call of the senses leads to in the end."

Then Yayati says, "May I ask you another boon? Won't you give me back my old age, which you have borne so valiantly? Won't you let me seek the rightful wisdom of my years?"

Once again, the exchange takes place. Puru becomes young, royal, magnificent, both inwardly and outwardly. After installing him as king, Yayati retires to the forest to spend the rest of his life in meditation.

Finally, he finds the fulfillment he was seeking in the realization of a spiritual joy the body can never attain.[2]

The Four Messengers

This message is underscored by another important story among the religions of the East, the story of Siddhartha Gautama and the Four Messengers. Siddhartha (the eventual founder of Buddhism) is born into the royal family in a small kingdom in modern-day Nepal. Shortly after his birth, the religious sages in the society foresee great things for him. He will become either an enlightened teacher or a world-conquering emperor. If he chooses the former, he will give up the kingdom in his indifference to worldly pleasure; and if the latter, he will defeat all his foes.

His father the king, while delighted to have such a son, is worried by the prophecy and hopes that his son will not be a world-renouncing ascetic. He tries to prevent it from coming to fruition by protecting his son from the difficulties of life and by satiating him with sensual pleasures. He does everything possible to see that all his son's needs are met and tended to within the royal apartments, free from any interface with the harsh realities of life in the world outside.

One day, however, Siddhartha resolves to go to the forest. His father organizes a pleasure party with lovely women, and orders that his son not see any sign of suffering on the road. The gods, however, decide to intervene in favor of the truth, and Siddhartha sees an old man walking along the side of the road. As he has never seen anyone suffering from the effects of old age before, he asks his charioteer the meaning of this sight. The charioteer explains that this is the visage of old age. Siddhartha inquires whether this will happen to him, too, and is assured that it will, indeed.

After returning home and pondering what he has seen, Siddhartha undertakes to leave the palace a second time. The king makes the same precautions, but once again the gods intervene and enable Siddhartha to see a man afflicted with illness, his body marked by disease. Learning from his charioteer what this is, Siddhartha asks if illness strikes all people. Hearing that it does, he again returns to the security of the palace.

He departs a third time, and again the king orders that he be shielded from any sign of suffering. This time the gods arrange for him to see a dead man being carried on a stretcher and followed by mourners. Looking to the charioteer for an explanation of what he is seeing, the prince is told the truth: that this is the final end of all human beings.

The charioteer proceeds to take Siddhartha to the forest where beautiful women await him, eager to provide him with every pleasure. The prince, however, deeply preoccupied with the realities of old age, sickness, and death, refuses their advances with a reflection on the impermanence of such pleasures and the sufferings they cause. This awareness will later become the first of the future Buddha's Four Noble Truths.

On a later occasion, the prince returns to the forest and is sitting in meditation when he is approached by a heavenly inhabitant disguised as a beggar. The beggar introduces himself to Siddhartha as a wandering ascetic who seeks truth for the sake of liberation, and as soon as he has finished speaking, he flies up to the sky. This brief visitation, however, provides Siddhartha with the insight he needs.

The first three messengers—old age, sickness, and death—express the problem of the human condition. The fourth messenger points the way to the solution: voluntary renunciation is the beginning of the path to liberation.[3]

I am subject to aging.
Aging is unavoidable

Gerontologists now recognize three stages of "old": the young old (65 to 74); the midrange old (75 to 84); and the oldest old (85 and above). These distinctions have become more meaningful with today's longer life spans, increased mobility, better care of physical needs, and more independence in financial matters. The three stages all share certain things in common, though there are also specific issues associated with each one. In the course of this chapter, we will reflect on some of the dynamics involved in each stage.

Demographers tells us that 18 percent of the population in the United States will be over sixty-five by 2020. When we "cross the line" ourselves, will we see it as a season in our lives where the spiritual dimension commonly increases even as the physical diminishes? Or will we see it as the passage from irrigated fields into a foreboding desert? We need to take a fresh look at the possibilities of this time in our lives. It is not necessarily the actual getting older that disturbs us, but the fear of what old age might bring that gives rise to an inner anxiety, as reflected in these lines by Sir Lawrence Brotherton.

As I go about life and living, every day I am confronted by older adults who sometimes seem confused, slow, or indifferent to social gestures. As I watch them getting in my way, it is easy to only see a wrinkled face, but never acknowledge them as real people. When I become impatient with them, reality slaps me in the face reminding me, as I am so they once were, and as they are, so I will be.

Some consider old age as an undesirable obstacle in their lives, believing it will never happen to us. I do not mind if it is God's will that I grow old, but when I am older, it upsets me to think others may perceive my doddering old age as defining who I am. Who I am will be explained by trembling hands spilling coffee, trying to move about with a walker, or the "oldest father" in church on Father's Day.

But that will not be the end of the story. Who I am will also be who I was. I was a military retiree, college graduate, teacher of handicapped children, state retiree, television producer, church denomination seminar presenter, Sunday school teacher, church van driver, deacon, short order cook, Coca-Cola routeman, salesman, truck driver, state hospital attendant, janitor, textile employee, husband, and father.

When the day comes and people look at me [and] only see a hindrance to their lifestyle, a number on a

Medicare card or supplementary insurance policy, will
you tell them who I was? They won't believe me.[4]

As we know, the society in which we live is based on the
ideology of strength and image, and no small amount of time,
energy, and money goes toward keeping these images intact! We
look forward to being eighteen, twenty-one, even thirty-five, but
who looks forward to being sixty-five? "Age," wrote Shakespeare,
"I do abhor thee; youth, I do adore thee."

While some are concerned about graying or thinning hair,
others are concerned about flexibility. Weight gain, too, is a concern, as our doctors urge us to change our eating habits, reminding us that as we age and the intensity level of our physical
activity decreases, we need fewer calories. It doesn't seem fair
that as our activities become more moderated, our appreciation
for food—especially for sweets—increases. As one person
remarked, "Who ever craved a piece of celery or a carrot stick?"

When I was living in New York City, one of my brothers
and his wife came to spend a few days with me over her birthday weekend. On the day of their departure, he said, "I still
haven't gotten a birthday present for her, so we're going out to
do some shopping." They visited several stores, and his wife
tried on various things, but nothing really grabbed her. They
were in Saks on Fifth Avenue and time was running out. As they
walked down the aisle of the store toward the door, a suave cos-
metic salesman standing by a display table that was spread with
special items importuned them, first to stop for a moment to
have a look, then to have the lady sit down while he applied
some of the latest wrinkle-removal crème beneath her eyes from
a little vial.

Seeing it as his last chance for a birthday gift, my brother
enthusiastically affirmed its miraculous properties and said,
"We'll take it! How much?"

Looking him in the eye, the salesman replied without
blinking: "Four hundred dollars." Too stunned to remind the
salesman of the truth brought home by the First Messenger, my
brother did the gallant thing as a sign of his appreciation for his
wife (who, truth be told, was not all that excited about the

crème). But when he came back and recounted the tale to me, it was with a distinct incredulity in his voice at how anyone could charge that much for two little vials of crème in a box. "It's not the *crème*," I said to him, laughing, "but what it hopefully *does* that one pays for: removing the *wrinkles!*"

On a deeper level, it isn't just a matter of readjusting our image of ourselves, but of accepting that we are subject to the law of impermanence and that law includes gradual changes along the way. We can't run or think as fast. We have less strength and stamina. Our coordination, memory, sexual appetite may diminish. The color of our hair changes and, yes, we develop wrinkles under our eyes. We come to see ourselves as others see us: as getting older.

On another occasion, I came home from the East Coast and my sister from the West Coast to spend the Christmas holidays with our parents. One of the hometown holiday events is my high school alma mater's basketball tournament, so when the finals came around and our team was in it, we all decided to get in the car and go to the game. My dad pulled up in front of the gym and said, "You go in and get the tickets while I park the car." So my sister and I stood in line, chatting, and when we got up to the table where tickets were being sold, I said "Two senior and two adult tickets, please." There was a brief moment of silence as the high school student eyed us and then, in his most courteous voice, said, "We could make that four senior tickets if you like...." My sister (at the time fifty-eight and two years my senior) and I looked at one another with surprise and burst out laughing. It was the first time either of us had been put in the "senior category" and it served us notice: we were aging and others saw it.

What must be transformed now is not so much how we look to other people, but how we ourselves look at life. This is the season of our lives when we begin to come to terms with ourselves, when we look more deeply within and find more strength in the spirit than in the flesh.

The Difference between Knowledge and Wisdom

While facelifts and every other kind of lift play into the cult of youthfulness and tend to reduce beauty to good looks, real beauty is the light that comes from the soul. In some cultures still, old people are seen as people of great wisdom, and there is immense respect for elders. Because they have lived long and deeply, they are accredited with understanding or intuition.

This is different from "knowing." Ours is a culture obsessed with and flooded by information. There is so much information available to us about everything. But this information tends to move on the level of "head" knowledge. There's too much of it for us to absorb or process.

And there lies the difference between knowledge and wisdom. Wisdom comes from the things that you deeply *realize*. Wisdom is a deeper way of knowing and involves the art of living in rhythm with your soul. This kind of knowing does not come just by reading another book or taking another course. It comes from the experience of living. These ideas and understanding have taken a lifetime to develop and cannot be simply replaced by something "new." They are held deeply in the soul.

Wisdom involves integration, the gathering together of the separate experiences of a lifetime, the suffering and the joy. Now our role is to authentically live what we have discovered about life, revealing in the use of our time and energy and material resources what we know to be important and what is not. It involves the linking of one's whole life together in a new and deeper kind of unity. The phases of old age are not when we stop growing, but the time in which we have the opportunity to grow in new ways.

The aged in our midst have a special gift to give because what they offer is born of experience and reflection, and people in our society have less time for reflection than almost any other culture in the world. It is the older generation, then, who are best placed to show another way to live. To be the truth-tellers and prophets. To lift up what is of value that we are in the process of losing or have already lost. To refocus ideals when they have been relegated to the shadows. The elderly are freer now than ever before to serve in these ways, because they stand to lose neither power nor status nor money.

The seasons of our lives are often correlated with the seasons of the natural world. Autumn becomes the metaphor for aging. It's a time in our lives when the fruits of our experience are beginning to be harvested. The blessings of this season receive too little attention. Aging is not just about losing strength and stamina; it's also about bringing together the fragments of varied experiences in our lives and holding them as one, of seeing now in retrospect the Providence that was guiding us. If aging is seen not just as the diminishment of the body but as the harvest time for the heart and for the soul, then it can be a time of rich reflection, inner strength, and confidence.

Youth, it has been said, is wasted upon the young. Their energy and drive are characterized by a restlessness that makes it difficult for them to simply, fully, *be* in the place and the time where they actually are. They're too stressed and rushed. Multitasking, the virus of our time, increases the difficulty of simply being present to what is, giving our full attention to it, and experiencing some joy or delight in engaging with it. Among the graces of aging is that there is more stillness, more solitude. One has the time to look through the personal and familial archives of photos, to savor the joyous times and reflect on the sad times. One can let both the successes and the personal failures pass by in review, and be grateful for them all because the whole of it has been a purveyor of wisdom.

Toward the end of his life, the medical doctor Paul Tournier once reflected that the renouncements of aging are in the order of action, not in the order of the heart and spirit. They are in the order of "doing," not in the order of "being." One lives in another manner; one does not live less. Life is different, but it remains fully *life*, with its petals even more open to the sun than before. Interest in the world does not lessen and it sometimes even grows. This distinction offers a perspective on aging that will reappear again and again in these pages.

We can live intensely even while advancing in age. If there are certain "minuses," there are also certain "pluses." We only lose one thing to acquire another. There are aspects of life to discover in aging that we could not have known earlier on.

Retirement

When your position is changed or your job comes to an end or your company leaves you no choice but to retire, then you are face to face with the questions: What does my life mean now? What remains to me now that I am too old to apply elsewhere?

Retirement has nothing to do with whether we work or not. It relates to the kind of work we will do and our reasons for doing it. This may be the first time in our lives when we are really free to choose work that brings out what is best and deepest in us, and at the same time evokes what is of value and worth cultivating in the world around us. Far from freeing us from our responsibilities to be active collaborators in creating a just and humane world, retirement opens the doors to new possibilities. Our financial situation may or may not require some remuneration for our time and effort. In any case, money is not the only standard for determining whether something is worth doing.

So the question becomes: What work will we do? The answer to that question usually becomes clear by tuning in to what the needs are around us.

When my father retired at sixty-two, I remember him saying, "Now I can devote myself to a number of things that are really important to me." He became the coordinator of Renew, a three-year program for parish renewal, for four of the parishes in our town. He served in a tri-state area as governor of the Serra Clubs, a Catholic association of professional people who support and promote vocations to church ministry. He became, after the necessary training, a volunteer in the national Guardian ad Litem program, working for the county as a legal counselor and advocate for young people. He worked with the School Sisters of Notre Dame in their fund-raising projects and served on the board of directors for the diocesan seminary. And he brought communion to the sick in the hospital. A plaque my sister gave him at his retirement, which he hung on the wall of his home office, said it well: "Retirement—when you stop making a living and start making a life."

In the very first year of his retirement, Dad came up with a way of deepening his relationship with his children and grandchildren and, at one and the same time, of deepening our own relationships with one another. It was a weekly family newsletter titled "Dad's Monday Morning Message"—or, as it came to be known in the family, the MMM. He devised official stationery for it. In the upper left corner was a checkerboard box, evocative of the Ralston Purina Company he had worked for, with a value-laden inscription in each box:

Think Tall: Keen, Alert Minds
Smile Tall: Sincere and Friendly Personalities
Stand Tall: Physical Vigor and Good Health
Live Tall: Character, Honesty, Religion

In the middle at the top was an outline of North America, with lines running out from my parents' home in Minnesota to all the other places where family members were located. And underneath the checkerboard and the continental outline, in a bar running across the page, was the injunction:

Aspire Nobly   *Adventure Daringly*   *Serve Humbly*

It became a family institution. The newsletter usually ran a couple of pages long. It was filled with what was going on in the lives of the various family members, and it always ended with an inspirational reflection. He sent it out in hard copy every week for eighteen years (we kids kept them in large, thick, three-ring binders), until the advent of computers rendered that method of publication obsolete. My brothers, my sister, and I chipped in, bought him a computer, and taught him how to use it—and the MMM went digital. Week in and week out, over twenty-six years until shortly before his death, my father devoted time to keeping the lines of communication open in all directions within the growing family of his children and grandchildren and great-grandchildren. It was definitely life-giving for him, but it was also a gift to us all.

He was an icon of an aging adult modeling the way to fullness of life. He enabled the younger generation to see that aging was not something to fear, to resist. Rather, he made it a bright and vibrant phase in life to be in. The seniors among us are the only ones who can do that. Failure to do so means consigning a quarter of our lives to the waste bin.

Researchers have shown that only 5 percent of those over sixty-five are in special-care institutions, and that 80 percent of the rest of the older population have no limitations in managing the rigors of daily living. While they do have more chronic illnesses, they also have fewer acute illnesses than younger people, as well as fewer injuries in the home and fewer accidents on the highway. And with the growing emphasis on gerontology as the baby-boomer generation ages, these rates are decreasing as well.[5]

Other cultures have ascribed to their venerable ones various roles and titles: the elder, the shaman, the sannyasi, the bodhisattva, the tzaddik, the sage. In our culture, we unfortunately do not have a formal title for those who are in this role for us, but more than ever we need them to assume it and to pass on what they have learned to those who come after them.

Their values, humor, spirituality, devotion to family, love of the outdoors, music, games, and wisdom sayings will be remembered far beyond their career status and salary level. Will the young of today, who are scanning for radar to guide their lives and decisions, find inscribed in our living the compass bearings that point the way to happy, fulfilled lives?

The Dynamics of Aging

We all have some stereotypical images of aging deeply imbedded in our psyches that might invite us to think that it is something to be avoided. So we allow ourselves to be invaded by fear and dread. We all can also think of some people we know who have lived long and aged gracefully, and we hope that we too will be able for yet many years to live as we are accustomed. Even though we may do all the things recommended to delay the process of growing old, we will nonetheless not be able to exercise complete control over what that stage of life will be for us.

Aging is obviously a difficult subject. A survey in 2007 by AARP (formerly the American Association of Retired Persons) found that nearly 70 percent of adult children have not talked to their parents about issues related to aging.[6] Some children avoid this most intimate of conversations because they believe their parents don't want to talk about it. Others think they know what their parents want. And some simply don't want to face the very real truth that if you are lucky enough to have parents who live well into their senior years, chances are good that disease, injury, frailty, even loneliness will affect their well-being.

There is no such thing as "one" conversation about aging, of resolving the future in one afternoon of talk. It's a process that can extend over thirty or more years because there are several delicate passages to negotiate: the loss of one's professional identity; the departure of one's children; a new role to define vis-à-vis one's spouse; the arrival of grandchildren; the decline of strength and energy; the necessity of finding a better-adapted place to live; the illness or death of loved ones; the confrontation with solitude; and finally, the facing of death itself.

In encountering these challenges, each one of us will react differently, formed by our character, our faith, our environment, our possibilities. Here are five suggestions for orienting yourself.

1. Maintain a Positive Vision of Yourself

The transition from one stage of life to another will not necessarily have a negative impact upon us. It depends on how we view it. In other words, it's not change itself, but our attitude toward it. Do we see our existence now as being "put on the shelf" or "in dry dock" until our body wears out? Or do we see ourselves in a new, liberating stage of life where we can now make a positive contribution to the lives of others in a variety of ways that were previously not possible to us?

The psychologist Erik Erikson suggested that elderly persons will find an interior equilibrium if they can accept life such as it has been, without excessive regrets. If they have too many unrealized dreams or dashed hopes, they risk sliding into despair and cynicism in the face of the remaining years. If their self-esteem was previously built principally upon beauty, influence, and work, they must now become aware that they are worth more than their accomplishments.

It is no longer about power and control, and we no longer have to prove ourselves anymore and try to get ahead. Titles and the climb up the social ladder are all behind us. There are parts of ourselves that are still awaiting recognition, that have gone wanting during the years when we had to be productive and responsible. A whole new world is opening before us in which we can learn to cook or take voice lessons or volunteer our services.

We must identify in ourselves whatever gives us a personal place in the world around us, for example: I'm a good neighbor. I'm a reliable helping hand for the local charitable organization. I enjoy social gatherings. I love music and dancing and am fun to be with. I'm an avid reader and book-club member. I have various roles in my local church community.

It is important that we choose to begin a new kind of life, a life that, while being related to the past, is full of its own promise and possibility. We must see what we do in this new phase of our lives as good, and we must find it life-giving for ourselves as well as for others. God has in mind another kind of usefulness for us.

For believers, the affirmation of faith—that the unconditional love of God is the source and end of our lives—is put to the test like never before. It is easier to believe when we are able to respond to this love with many activities and gratifying relationships in our lives as manifestations of God's love. It's when we sit alone and inactive that we see whether our spiritual lives are strong enough to provide us with sense and hope.

2. Reread Your Personal History

An elderly person naturally turns toward the past. The time is ripe to reread one's history, to find meaning in one's experiences, and to perhaps upgrade the image that one has had of oneself. This is the season for sitting back and asking ourselves what contribution the various experiences in our personal history have made to the mosaic of our lives. We will surely become aware of interests and qualities whose nurture and development were stunted. Now is the time to carry them forward. This is not the time when we stop growing, but the period in which we strive to make sense of the pattern of growth across the whole of our lives, and the time when we get to be more of who we've always been.

This assessment is not easy work. Were our lives marked by a recognizable continuity and consistency of development? Were there some core values that kept weaving their way through the tapestry of our years? Who are we after all these years? Such a taking stock often requires the testimony of witnesses who are not in any way invested in the outcome. The task requires great humility and unerring truthfulness with neither idealization nor severe judgment. Undertaking such a process of reflecting on one's life is the price of inner peace.

To reread one's life in this manner, self-compassion is indispensable, making it possible to acknowledge errors and impasses without making light of them. We see more clearly how, at the time, we did not have the wherewithal to do otherwise; how we were lacking in maturity, emotional objectivity, personal experience, and other qualities or resources. This same humility enables us to recognize that, because of our shortcomings, others—even those closest and most dear to us—suffered, sometimes deeply, without our intending it.

This rereading also brings out all the blessings of our journey, all the reasons to be grateful. We recall the people and resources that enabled us to make it through the dark and difficult times. We find a pathway winding through our life, leading us over, under, and around the obstacles that rose up before us. We experience forgiveness for our deviations, willful and otherwise, and can express our gratitude at finding our way back onto the road that has led us to today. We become reconciled with others, with our past, with ourselves, and with God.

Remembering in this manner all the ground traversed, all the difficulties surmounted, all the help received along the way, provides the inner resources for facing with confidence and trust the ultimate frontier of passing from this life into the next.

3. Face the Limitations and Losses Associated with Becoming Old

The number of those for whom physical loss is a major feature of the aging process is significantly lower than we tend to think. Studies indicate that the rates of disability are declining steadily, and recovery from acute disabilities improves from year to year. The number of elderly who are healthy is increasing at rates never seen before. This plays an important part in what makes the elderly currently the fastest-growing constituency in the American population. The data also reveals that the decrepitude and incapacitation that come with age are present, on average, only about the last three months of one's life. Even then, studies indicate, mental clarity is more likely than not to remain to the end. We have a lot of life left to live.[7]

That said, there are nonetheless still many adults who witness their parents' mental degeneration and varying degrees of memory loss, or spouses whose partners no longer seem to be themselves or who become like children again. Even when we are spared these more serious disabilities, there are increasing limitations. We may no longer jog or even walk as fast as we once did. We may get in and out of a car more carefully. We no longer lift heavy objects like we once did. But these limitations are boundaries, not barriers. They limit us, but they do not stop us unless we decide to allow them to stop us. As in the case of a blind person who develops more acute hearing, or a deaf person who learns to read lips, our limitations in one area may simply find us giving further development to our capabilities in another. We will do better to see our limitations as an aspect of everyone's life, albeit in different ways, than to allow ourselves to be defined by them.

Old age is a school of life. As we move from being "young olds" to "midrange olds" to the "oldest olds," we will, little by little, learn to let go: first of our different professional roles; then of colleagues and friends; and perhaps eventually of spouse, home, apartment, and even autonomy. It is not always possible to count on friends or a spouse for those little services like applying ointment to one's back or helping to tie a shoe. These various successive losses remind us that life is fragile; they remind us to live more and more fully in the present moment.

It is no longer what we possess or have accumulated that counts, but what is passing that is perceived as precious. It is no longer a question of amassing goods but of giving them to others who can put them to good use. And when we are among the "oldest old," it's more than ever a time when everything passes or disappears. But each of these passages, of these transitions, of these present moments is precious precisely because of its fleeting nature rather than its permanence.

Finally, these lessons that life imposes about where true security lies, what constitutes real happiness and fulfillment, contribute to deepening our relationship with God and serve to prepare us for the big "letting go" that will be our death.

4. Little by Little, Accept Depending on Others and Not Just on Yourself

Learning this is particularly difficult for those of us who, for diverse reasons, are accustomed to taking care of things by ourselves. Autonomy, whether driving or walking or preparing our own meals, is one of the things we cherish most dearly. Clinging to it when we no longer have alertness or flexibility can become a new source of suffering. It is a lesson we must inevitably learn. The fruit of this learning is to one day consent to letting go, to accept that we are no longer in control, and to gratefully receive what is given.

As we age, the real task of life and love is to continually hand over, without bitterness, regret, or envy, all the things that were once so much our own: power, attention, popularity, usefulness, turf of every sort. It's something we will have to work at.

Disability, inactivity, hopelessness, helplessness, anger at being dependent, and even feelings of worthlessness are the stuff of depression. Resistance to aging thrives on the assumption that somehow this should not be happening to *me*. But aging is a part of life. It calls forth from us a new level of honesty, openness, and willingness to face the inevitable. While we do not get to choose when or how we are going to die, we can decide how we are going to live.

A good strategy is to cultivate friendships not only with those of our own age, but also with those who are both younger and older than ourselves. We can draw upon the wisdom and experience of our seniors and learn from their coping skills. And since one of the least attractive aspects of aging is the feeling that one is no longer up to date, younger friends can serve as mentors and coaches to keep us in the game with digital technology that enables us to stay connected.

The aged person is no longer defined by possessions, but by this new capacity to receive gracefully what is offered. One enters into a gratuitous world where everything is given and nothing is owed. In the ordinariness of daily life, this experience can open to a deepening of the spiritual life in which one simply allows oneself to be cared for.

We are called at this time in our lives to bless others, especially the young, by admiring their energy, beauty, and achievement without envy or bitterness. This involves saying what John the Baptist said when Jesus appeared: "He must increase and I must decrease."

5. Discover the Meaning of Life and Continue to Savor It

Do we not already begin to age from the very first day of our lives? Aging, in this sense, could be synonymous with growing up, with reference to a kind of growth that is not finished with one's professional retirement, but continues with an active life until one's last breath. We are never finished growing, because each experience of life, whether easy or difficult, happy or unfortunate, applies a new stroke of the brush to the work that we are.

So we could say that there is a future in aging. Even when it looks like diminishment, we are always evolving and becoming.

People do not grow old; they are old when they stop growing. To "grow" is not a question of size, but a question of depth and meaning. As is the case with literature, the sense of a line or a chapter or a book can only be discovered when we have written the last chapter of the book, the last line of the last chapter, the last letter of the last word.

It is the same with our lives. As in a book, there are surprise developments, the introduction of new themes, the playing out of paradox. Each stage can be read and interpreted for itself, but we have to wait till the end to see how all these threads come together. This dynamic of unifying the parts is what makes growing old a time of wisdom and of grace.

Rather than seeing ourselves as the passive victims of our inner and outer worlds, as helpless and weak, we acknowledge that we are responsible agents and can make choices. We do not have all the answers, and we learn to tolerate ambivalence. We seek the company of other thriving people. We can pursue and enjoy pleasure, and at the same time look at and live through our pain. We have learned to distinguish between reality and fantasy, and are able to live with reality. We come to terms with our limitations, flaws, and imperfections. We confront the many losses that come into our lives over time. We become adept at finding in every experience opportunities for creative transformation.

One of aging's better gifts is that time becomes more meaningful. We are always aware of it. The experiences we live are not taken for granted but are savored; every layer of them is wrung out and relished. There is no time to waste anymore. The *now* is no longer one moment on the way to something else, but is the gift package just received and we want to unwrap it and enjoy it. When we ease into moments with that kind of passion, appreciation, and glee, we have become more fully alive to the richness in living that has been there all the time, but we missed it because we were going too fast. All of life's preceding periods feel like practice for this time. It is only in the present that we learn to live, and it is the present that is increasingly the focus of our later years.

When we can no longer walk as fast, we are more likely to appreciate the flowers along the way, hear the birdsong, and stop to talk. The young, it is said, are always on their way to somewhere else and are filled with wanting. A feature of age is less interest in the going and the striving and more appetite for being, for simply living.

This period may prove to be fully a quarter to a third of our lives. It is not a period without purpose. The attitude with which we approach this time will make a difference in whether we are able to mine its potential richness. It is a time for self-reflection, yes, but even more, for self-transcendence. It is the period in our lives when everything we have learned up to now can be put at the service of others. It is a time when we can make of our lives a gift to the world around us.

Resources for Your Inner Work

Reflections

1. Write down the things you repress, resist, or resent that are happening in your body as a result of aging, the things that cause you to grow panicky or depressed.
2. Look for an opportunity to speak openly and plainly about these things with someone you know as a way of freeing yourself from the prison of your resistance and fear, and as a way of growing in your acceptance of the simple truth of what is.
3. Title a sheet of paper "What I Cling to," and then proceed to list what comes to mind (for example, my independence, a self-image that is no longer reflective of reality, any particular material good, and so on).

Reread Your Personal History

1. Acknowledge errors and impasses without making light of them.
2. Create a litany of blessings, all your reasons to be grateful.

3. Reflect on the pathway winding through your life, leading you through the challenges and difficulties along the way to where you are today.
4. Look for any others, of yourself or your own story, that still want reconciliation and forgiveness.

Exercise for a Discussion Group

1. Invite everyone to take a few minutes to quietly reflect on the manifestations of aging that they observe within themselves.
2. Then, invite each person to speak and to preface what he or she chooses to say with, "I am subject to aging. Aging is unavoidable." Encourage people to lighten up and laugh by "telling on themselves," revealing the games they play to hide the truth and prolong the illusion to themselves and others that they will be forever young, energetic, flexible— forever possessed of a thick head of dark hair, and so on.
3. Invite everyone to reflect on the opportunities they have now—in whatever phase of the aging process they may be in—that they did not have before in the same measure.
4. Then, invite everyone to identify some of these opportunities and to share whether they have yet begun to engage with them and, if so, what the benefit for others and/or the effect upon their own inner life has been.

Poem

The Temples of Agrigento

The pile of pillars lying pell-mell in pieces
once stood proud and permanent
on the brow of the hill, marble-covered
columns, chiseled and gleaming
in Mediterranean light.

Six men with hands joined could not encircle
this section of column thrusting upward

from the rubble, only one of thirty-four
moved into place by some marvel
of ropes and pulleys to hold aloft
a roof over the temple of Zeus.

These stones have endured the hammers
and been pulled by the horses
of Phoenicians, Carthaginians, Romans, and Greeks;
provided prayerful sanctuary
for Moors bowing towards Mecca
and Norman knights towards the cross.

And now, scattered like fallen giants
in fields of wild grass, Sunday strollers zig-zag
among them, reading in their large script
a reminder that the page on which they
presently step will soon be turned by
the finger of time.

What path, then, do you choose to walk
with your short and treasured life?

Will to Live

While sitting on the porch
I saw a pine warbler
try to fly through
the picture window.

The thud made me start
from my chair as it
                    dropped
to the shingled wall
                    below
caught an edge
      it could hold

and then hung back
like a child dangling
its full body weight
from one twiggy leg
on the jungle jim bar
with arms hanging down.

And I realized that I too
had stopped
                    breathing
expecting any second
to see that tiny claw
      open

and the yellow-brown form in
>   f

>   r

>   e

>   e

>   f

>   a

>   l

>   l

But the little one hung longer
than I could hold my breath and
—to my astonishment—
with a spasmic shake of the head
like one emerging from a bad dream
released its grasp and fluttered
weakly to the ledge below
where it sat
>   huddled in a corner

calling back
its life force.

O how things want to live! I thought
and suddenly found
within the image of
>   that feathered form

hanging by a claw
>   from the siding of the house

the courage within myself
to face the challenge of the day.

Chapter Two

Illness

Certainly, the ways we respond to illness are numerous, extremely varied, and impossible to foresee: we may experience dejection, rebellion, denial, bitterness, but other possible outcomes of illness are simplification, discovery of what is essential in life, refinement, and purification. In our illness we are called to accept responsibility for "assigning a meaning" to our suffering.

—Enzo Bianchi

We live in a health-obsessed society and see disease as something that shouldn't be happening, when actually it's just a natural part of being human, of finding ourselves in a body that is changing and not entirely under our control.

Illness is an experience that reveals to us that our life is marked by loss as well as gain, and is built on acceptance of our limitations and vulnerabilities as well as of our strengths. When we are sick, we have fewer possibilities, but one of the possibilities we do have is to face in a more direct way the questions life places before us: What is my worth? What meaning does life have? What is the meaning of the suffering and losses with which life is filled? In its own way, illness invites us to return to what is essential.

Everyone appreciates good energy and health, and none of us *wants* to get sick. When we do, the situation of illness presents us with an opportunity to practice letting go and to look at things more deeply.

A friend of mine who pastored the cathedral in Cuernavaca, Mexico, invited me to come down for a week's holiday. He said he would take some time off and show me some of the beautiful and interesting areas around the region. But on my first day there I ate some bad food, was hit with food poisoning, and spent the rest of the week sitting in my friend's backyard garden. As recounted in this poem, while my visit there turned out to be very different than anticipated, it was not without its own blessings.

More Than Enough

I came
running on empty,
from sea-level snowflakes
to sun-baked, thin mountain air.

I came
to visit a good friend,
discover the meaning of siesta,
and roll some tortillas and beans.

I learned of Cortez and his conquest,
read murals of the Indians' sad slavery,
and was early laid low
by Montezuma's revenge.

Now peacefully sequestered
behind eucalyptus-hedged garden walls,
what was most needed is providentially given—
a time and place just to be.

It is more than enough
to be awakened by the songbird's full-throated warble
and the soft, gentle caress
of a Mexico morning breeze.

It is more than enough
to fill up the lungs
with the sweet smell of orange blossoms
freshly perfuming the air.

It is more than enough
to open my eyes to wine-red bougainvilleas
and flame tree buds bursting
in April's translucent early light.

It is more than enough
to be greeted through the window
by a carnival of blossoms
dancing to daylight in terra cotta pots.

It is more than enough
to drink from the harvest
of grapefruit and orange trees
hanging heavy with encasements of liquid gold.

For another time
save the street noise and vendors,
the acrid smell of diesel fuel
in narrow city streets.

For another time
save the ancient Aztec stones
and the sun god's bludgeoning hammer
on mid-day hikers' heads.

For this time,
the little universe
behind the garden gate
is more than enough.

I am not trying to romanticize the experience of illness with poetry. I recognize there is a big difference between being laid low by food poisoning for a few days and having to deal with a chronic or even permanent condition. But what is true in both short- and long-term illness is that it presents us with an opportunity to look at things more deeply. While it is not something we ever go looking for or even welcome in its visitation, it can yield its own valuable insight. In the story of Siddhartha

Gautama, illness is the Second Messenger, reminding us that everything passes.

As we know, our physical self is impermanent and is constantly changing in unexpected ways. We have control over some conditions that affect the body, but not over others. Part of wisdom is to be able to discern the difference. You can get a surgeon to fix your shoulder or your knee or your hip, but in the end each will go the way of all created things. Everything deteriorates in the end and falls apart.

The care we exercise for our physical health might even increase our resistance relative to accepting our mortality: "Here I am, making my way to the fitness center several times a week, working on my abs and my muscle mass, keeping my heart healthy and my weight down, and you're telling me it's all for naught in the end?" Good health can also be something on which we hitch our happiness, something we cling to, an attachment like any other.

This of course does not mean that we stop watching what we eat and cease exercising regularly. We are to do the best we can to take good care of what we have been given, but at the same time recognize its impermanence and accept that we only have so much control over it.

Karen's Story

In a health-care apartment building in New York City, a woman lies on her back in bed. Her name is Karen. In 1989, at twenty-two years of age and fresh out of college, she developed a severe pain in her right shoulder along with crippling fatigue. She went to the doctor. The pain soon spread to her left shoulder, then to her knees and hips.

The doctors gave her cortisone shots for the pain, but no one connected the pain with her fatigue. This went on for several years. At work, her colleagues continued to cover for her, writing notes for her when her hands were too sore. When the cortisone shots failed to work, the doctors recommended surgery. The subsequent operation revealed a number of torn ligaments in her shoulder.

Eventually, Karen had to resign from her job and move in with her father and his sister for what she hoped would be her recovery. Just a few years earlier, she was a National Merit Scholar attending Yale University, as well as a dedicated clarinet player. She ran five miles a day and lifted large stacks of plates as part of her job in the college dining hall. Now she couldn't turn on the television set without help. Let her describe the rest herself:

> Six years later, I was finally diagnosed with Lyme disease. At first I was hopeful that with a new verdict, there would be a cure. I didn't realize that treatment often increased the painful symptoms. Moreover, I couldn't tell if the treatment was working.
>
> Then the doctors decided I now had post-Lyme syndrome and put me on steroids. That made everything worse, and I became more disabled: I couldn't walk from one side of the room to the other. I could hardly speak. I couldn't feed myself. I felt helpless. I couldn't fight it. In the past, I saw myself as a fighter. I was used to dealing with challenges, but this challenge overwhelmed me. I went into a deep depression and wanted to die.
>
> I was angry at God. I thought I had done everything right. I worked hard. I exercised and took care of my body. I stayed away from alcohol and drugs. And now I was helpless. I felt isolated. The medical system had failed me. Churchgoing had failed me.
>
> Some of my friends from work and some from college stuck with me. Over time, my blessings became more apparent to me, but not until the last five or six years.
>
> I got back in touch with the Church through my godmother's encouragement. I agreed to allow a priest come see me to keep her happy. In my first visit with him, I burst out with all of my problems with the Church. He just listened, without judging. He came by often after that, just to visit, and it became a joy to talk to him. A sister from the church also starting bringing holy communion. I began to think about things in a different way.
>
> When the first priest was transferred, another one picked up where he left off. I have learned from him that a spiritual recovery can be just as important as a physical recovery. "Nothing is wasted," he said, inviting me to offer up

my pain for someone else that needed help. At first I couldn't offer it up for anyone who was in better shape than I was. Children in certain parts of Africa are starving and sick with AIDS. Some of them are orphans, who receive little medical care, and have no roof over their heads. I offered up my pain for them. It began to feel less heavy.

Today, I try to not think so much about my illness. I focus instead on what makes me happy. I have been trying alternative treatments, and I feel less pain. Now there are times when I can write and pay a bill, walk across the room, and feed myself. I see people more and that helps. When you hear about other people's lives, that takes you out of yours.

Now instead of looking at what I have lost, I try to see how much better I've gotten since those worst days. I have a little more control. I have my own place. I need aides to help me every day, but I'm still on my own.

The hardest thing is not having freedom. I need to depend upon others. I hold on to little things that others give me: a prayer, or an idea that suffering is never wasted because it can get transformed into something positive for someone or something else. So I offer up my shoulder pain for better relations with Iran and my sore knee for North Korea to come to its senses.

Today I feel the only thing I can control in this life is what goes on in my head. I do what I have to do to take care of my body and try to let the rest go. It's all about not trying to control what you can't control. I try not to think too much about the future or the past. I try to think about what I can do right now to feel better; perhaps call a friend or watch a movie.

I see my life as a journey to find out who I am and how my life can have meaning even without the external evidence of what society would think of as accomplishments, be it career, family, financial security, or hobbies. On those days when the pain is bearable, I'm grateful for what I have and welcome the love of my friends. That's what I value the most.

Claiming Our Most Intimate Dependency

Pain is part of life. By and large we live by the pleasure principle: do what feels good and avoid what doesn't. Few have to deal with the kind of chronic pain of which Karen speaks, but a certain amount of pain is unavoidable—especially in relation to the first two Messengers: aging and illness. If we can stand and face them instead of fleeing in fear, we will handle them better. Everything is made easier through acquaintance. In becoming acquainted and learning to live gracefully with small pains, we will learn how to live patiently with larger ones.

Illness and pain are effective teachers because they reveal to us the truth of the impermanence of our physical body. Sooner or later, we all age. We all have to face the possibility of difficult and debilitating conditions like rheumatoid arthritis, osteoporosis-related fractures, and illness. We all have to face the eventuality of our own death. What will be our anchor or inner wellspring, a source of equanimity under trial?

The much-loved spiritual writer Henri Nouwen recounted what happened inside him after he was hit by a car and brought to the hospital with a ruptured spleen. The doctor told him he wasn't sure that he would make it through surgery. But he did, and in the hours lived both before and after the operation, lying bound by straps on a table and surrounded by masked figures, he was struck by this insight:

> I suddenly experienced my complete dependency. Not only did I realize that I was fully dependent on the skills of an unknown medical team but that my deepest being was a dependent being. I knew with certainty that had nothing to do with any particular human insight that, whether I survived the surgery or not, I was safely held in a divine embrace and would certainly live….
>
> All at once I knew that all human dependencies are embedded in a divine dependency and that divine dependency makes dying part of a greater and vaster

way of living. This experience was so real, so basic and so all-pervasive, that it radically changed my sense of self and affected profoundly my state of consciousness for years to follow.

There is a strange paradox here: dependency on people often leads to slavery, but dependency on God, when lived in trust, leads to freedom. When we know that God holds us safe—whatever happens—we don't have to fear anything or anyone but can walk through life with great confidence....

When we claim our most intimate dependency on God, not as a curse but as a gift, then we can discover the freedom of the children of God....When we can reach beyond our fears to the One who loves us with a love that was there before we were born and will be there after we have died, then sickness, injury, and even death will be unable to take away our freedom.

Once we have come to the deep inner knowledge—a knowledge more of the heart than of the mind—that we are born out of love and will die into love, that every part of our being is deeply rooted in love and that this love is our true Father and Mother, then all forms of evil, illness and death lose their final power over us and become painful, but also hopeful, reminders of our true divine childhood.[1]

Henri Nouwen spent the last ten years of his life living in L'Arche communities, which had been founded by Jean Vanier for persons suffering from mental and physical disabilities. (*L'Arche* is French for "the ark," referring to Noah's ark, which provided a place of safety for the endangered.) Both Jean and Henri repeatedly witnessed to how sickness and injury, which we fear and tend to see as a curse, seem to be favored instruments in God's toolbox.

In the Gospel of Luke, we read:

After leaving the synagogue [Jesus] entered Simon's house. Now Simon's mother-in-law was suffering from a high fever, and they asked him about her. Then he stood over her and rebuked the fever, and it left her. Immediately she got up and began to serve them. As the sun was setting, all those who had any who were sick with various kinds of diseases brought them to him; and he laid his hands on each of them and cured them. (Luke 4:38–40)

We should not miss in this passage that the occasion for people's meeting Jesus and experiencing his power was their infirmity. One only need think of Ignatius Loyola, for example, the founder of the Jesuits, whose conversion came during a period of convalescence from a wound incurred in battle—or of Thérèse de Lisieux, the architect of the "little way" of holiness, who suffered from tuberculosis and died at twenty-four—to know that physical ailments not only pose no impediment to holiness but often seem to serve as trampolines into a deepening spiritual life.

Beth's Story

Beth is a wife, mother, and learning specialist who works with teachers to help them address the wide spectrum of learning styles in their classrooms. Over a period of several months, she experienced discomfort after eating and was having trouble digesting most foods. After several tests, the diagnosis was adenocarcinoma of the stomach (advanced cancer). The gastrointestinologist described the tumor as "as large as a child's fist," with the cancer at stage four. He recommended immediate surgery with the hope of palliative care, pending any prognosis for future treatment until after that time.

Beth said:

Standing on the sidewalk outside the doctor's office after that meeting felt surreal. A part of me wanted to call out to those passing by, "I'm dying of cancer. Can't you tell?" Another part couldn't absorb this news. This was happening to someone else; not me.

I prayed, phrases like, "Oh God—help me, help me be strong. Oh God—help me, help me be strong," over and over again.

As the plans for surgery and medical relief moved quickly forward, Beth assumed her death was right around the corner and wanted to prepare for it. She went to someone who she felt could help her by accompanying her through the final stage of her journey. She began reading a book about how to live as if you have only a year left. As she waited the week and a half between the diagnosis and the surgery, she focused on her inner spiritual life. Along with taking care of her personal and medical needs, she filled her days with reading and prayer. She had practiced meditation on and off over the past year, but now began to meditate every day for twenty minutes morning and evening. Even when she couldn't sit up, she meditated lying down.

She went through surgery, ten days in the hospital, six weeks of recovery, and then five months of chemotherapy and radiation. At one point, she landed back in the hospital with a fever and low blood count due to infection. Throughout it all, she prayed all the time—formal prayer, informal prayer, reading, and always meditation.

Over the next months, I came to live moment by moment, to savor the victories over my body and to appreciate, oh appreciate, my family and friends who gave so lovingly of their prayers and time.

After a year, with the odds still against me, I took a trip to a hospice where I planned to spend my final days. I felt reassured by this beautiful, sunny, and nurturing facility and filled out an application. I also went on a week-long retreat, "Savoring Life by Facing Our Mortality." At that retreat I wrote an eighty-page journal, "A Testimony of My Life," using a guideline provided by the facilitator. I hope to leave it for my daughters to read, but as an added bonus, I got to relive and process the highlights of my life so far and the paths going forward.

I wanted to travel and visit old friends across the country. So later in the year I took a five-month sabbatical from my job and did just that, keeping another journal of all the places I traveled during that period.

On one of these trips, I went to Texas with a close friend to visit another close friend. We were sitting on her porch late one morning, still in our pajamas, sipping coffee, and chatting the time away. Both friends looked at me, and one asked, "What do you think eternity will be like?" I knew my answer would be important to them because of my experience, but I hadn't given it a clear thought up to that point. "Like this perfect moment," I spontaneously responded. "Here we are, sitting together, next to this beautiful garden, laughing, sharing, enjoying. It will be like this, forever and ever."

We have millions of these perfect moments every day, and I continue to thank God for them. I pray the instant I wake up, on and off throughout the day, and the last moment before I fall asleep. I look for each day to be filled with meditation, reading, acts of kindness, acceptance, peace, and prayer.

Two years into recovery, I wrote in my Christmas message, "I have everything I need." This most simple and honest statement reflected my spiritual growth and renewed appreciation of the gift of God's love. It took the reality of facing the loss of life here on earth to truly understand that everything I need comes from God, and lo and behold, I have it already. Imagine! All we need is this moment with God. Nothing else matters.

Today, over six years later, I can honestly say this experience facing death represents the most important and unsurpassed experience in my life. It changed my life. My life on the outside hasn't changed all that much; but on the inside, oh my! *Inside* I experienced a profound and overwhelming evolution in my experience of God's love.

Of course, fear and anxiety are always waiting in the wings, ready to take the stage. The other day my oncologist said, "I know you. If I tell you that you are going to go through hell next Wednesday, you'll pull your resources together and face the challenge. But if I tell you I don't know what's going to happen, you'll go crazy." This is all about me wanting to be in control. I hope I can begin to let go of needing that clarity, but it's hard and will continue to challenge me.

Still, surviving after cancer is easier than I thought it would be. I think it's because I have a new and renewed appreciation of my blessings. I am learning to take it slow, accept what I cannot change, and trust in God. I also feel the embrace of those who love me, both the ones I see all the time and the ones I don't. There is so much love coming your way that you don't actively think about, but you can feel its embrace, and this is what I have felt since the day I was first diagnosed.

I have never been more alive than I am today.

As Beth's story witnesses, there is a deep Mystery at work in our lives, and our awareness of it intensifies in periods of trial where we come face to face with what Nouwen calls "our most intimate dependency."

True Healing

In the biography of Jean Vanier titled *The Miracle, The Message, The Story*, Vanier is described as running himself ragged trying to visit all the new L'Arche communities in Africa, India, Canada, the United States, and Honduras, and he ended up in a hospital for two months. During that time of quiet convalescence, he decided to step down as international coordinator of the communities and asked for a sabbatical year. He spent it living in one of the L'Arche houses for the most severely disabled—those who could not speak and who could barely move their inert limbs.

Jean's particular responsibility in the house to which he was assigned was to care for Eric, who was blind, deaf, unable to speak. Though poor in many ways, Eric was nonetheless extraordinarily rich in qualities of the heart. But Jean came to appreciate that in order to perceive and receive Eric's treasures, he himself would have to move into a slower pace of life, and become more attentive and ready to listen, more centered and contemplative. Eric, whose loneliness was reflected in the tension of his whole body and who relaxed only when he sensed that he was loved, called Jean to greater love.[2]

This, Vanier says, is the only healing that is true healing: the gradual opening up to other people in true relationship. And such, he is quick to add, is exactly what the mentally disabled teach us: to relate from the heart, to accept our own wounds and disabilities. So it is not only our own infirmities, but also our encounter with the limitations of others who are disabled or ill that can be a place of real inner healing and insight.

This inner healing is usually something that we discern with the passing of time. It is a work of the Holy Spirit, in the dark and out of sight. But one day, as we step back and reflect on our experience, we may suddenly become aware that we are seeing and responding to things from a different place within, and in that moment we recognize that an inner wound has healed.

When I served for several years as an ecumenical advisor to the L'Arche communities in North America, I heard the assistants state in various ways that while those whom they served had mental disabilities, "we assistants have emotional disabilities, and they are teaching us how to love, how to speak from the heart." This is another version of what Christian faith calls the paschal mystery. Not only in death is there life, but also in sickness there is healing—sometimes physical, sometimes emotional, sometimes psychological, sometimes spiritual. But *healing*.

Jean said:

> As I grow older, I am discovering more and more the *gift* of my own poverty and weakness. When we are strong, we can often do it alone. When we feel weaker, when we live loss and anguish, we are more aware of our need for God, for others, for community. And from the center of that awareness we open ever wider to the Source of healing, to the Source of saving grace.[3]

At the Heart of the Gospel

The first of the Beatitudes, it is said, encapsulates all the others: "Blessed are the poor in spirit, for theirs is the kingdom of God." Being "poor in spirit" means never losing sight of our neediness and our dependency upon God. As we age, we know in our heart of hearts of our own neediness, but we try to mask it rather than face it and live out of it. Life, however, continually conspires to unmask our illusions. The neediness is built in. It is not meant to be denied or run from. It is meant to turn us to God. And there are few things that more effectively de-mask us and strip away the layers of our self-sufficiency and independence than sickness. When we are sick, we are not in control, not in a position to call all the shots. Sickness makes us aware that we need God's help and mercy more than anything else. That is the whole point of the Beatitudes.

Once we have gotten the insight of, on the one hand, our utter neediness and dependency, and on the other hand, a God in whose love and care we are utterly safe, the result is truly blessed: a person with a patient and humble acceptance of what happens, a person who is able to live with a steadfast heart free from bitterness and fear. "Blessed are the poor in spirit, for theirs is the kingdom of heaven."

It's rare that we traverse an intense suffering or a grave illness without making God the object of a sorrowful interrogation: "Why do you allow this tragedy, this suffering?" It's a question that obliges us to revisit our notion of an "all-powerful God." How can one who is all-powerful not use that power to eradicate evil and suffering?

Gwendolyn, diagnosed with ovarian cancer, shares her experience of both the question and the answer:

In the darkest days I've had, between the last surgery and the last chemo, I finally felt angry about this cancer and all the impacts of it on my and our life. I remember ranting to my husband Richard at one point, through tears, that now I understood why Teresa of Avila shook her fist and yelled at God when her carriage was overturned in the stream: "No wonder you don't have many friends if this is how you treat them!" I'd just had enough of it all and didn't want to return to chemo treatments. I was so tired.

After my rant, Richard helped me lie down for a nap and I found myself silently confessing to God how I know he is my healer, my protector, my rock, my very source of life...Then it occurred to me that this was a psalm. The psalms are full of rants and emotional outpourings followed by the truths the psalmist still knows and believes, and then everything culminates in worship.

I realized that God is big enough to deal with my anger. God knows how I feel anyway, so expressing my feelings is really just being honest. What I experienced was a sense of love and peace, knowing that whatever I do or say, God will continue to love and treasure me just as and where I am. That's a pretty heartening and reassuring truth at any time, and especially in the midst of this journey with cancer!

Some of you may know the verse of scripture that tells us that "all things work together for good for those who love God" (Rom 8:28). Well, that is certainly happening to me right now. Suffice it to say that I am living life more fully, richly, and deeply than ever before. Never have I been so relaxed, felt so confident, trusted so easily, been so patient as I am now. The cancer stinks but what God is using it for is beautiful. Out of the ashes of this terrible disease is coming a new life. I know that I am not the person I was six months ago. My life will never be the same, neither will Richard's. But I have focus, purpose, a new understanding of my gifts, and a clear direction in a way I've never experienced before. For all this and more I give thanks and praise to God.

We find ourselves here at the heart of the paradox of Christian faith: it is in the acceptance and penetration of the profoundly human experiences of diminishment, weakness, humiliation, and dependency that God's power is found, expressed, and experienced. Here we are far from the power of a magician who could wave a magic wand and rearrange the world and our situation in it according to our desires. Rather, we enter into a much subtler dynamic wherein God endorses our human condition with the death of Jesus and through it opens up for us a path to life. Biblical hope is more than a vague belief that "all will work out well." Biblical hope in the light of Jesus' resurrection is the certainty that things finally have a victorious meaning no matter how they turn out.

It is often in the stripping of our autonomy through sickness that we are able to perceive this reality at work in all its intensity. We discover that our life is not a given and that good health is not a reality to which we have an inalienable right. We experience the gift of quality of life even more intensely and discover how joy can come in many forms and in the measure of our capacity to open to it and receive it.

This witness comes most often and most clearly from those battling with illness. On the eve of her fourth round of chemotherapy for breast cancer, Sue wrote to family and friends:

> It's been an interesting experience being diagnosed with cancer. As another survivor said, cancer is a word, not a sentence. But it's a word that makes you reevaluate everything in your life. You come to realize that some of the things that have kept you stressed and busy for so many years are not really very important after all.
>
> It's really too bad that we have to be hit over the head with a baseball bat like cancer before we slow down and realize what's truly important in life!
>
> People and our relationships with them are the treasures of our lives. Yet we spend so much time not being with the people who really matter to us. Trust me, those people and relationships are irreplaceable. You'll regret it forever if you don't tell them so now. So don't wait 'til you're diagnosed with cancer or something else...tell people that they matter to you. All we have is today: Celebrate it!

The Interior Quest

What galvanizes our time and energy in large measure? Work-related activities? An accumulation of material goods? A variety of charitable projects? Family? Illness, whether physical or psychological, reminds us that nothing is held permanently; everything is in transition. We will not die with our material goods, and we will eventually withdraw from our most profitable, entertaining, or altruistic activities.

But there is yet another path that leads to life—more demanding, to be sure, and perhaps, paradoxically, more costly: the interior quest, a spiritual path whose goal is communion with God, a life in which our fundamental intention is to encounter God. And the place of this encounter is within our own hearts, in that intimate, fragile, vulnerable place where we know that life is a gift. It is an encounter where we are open to more than just ourselves, turned toward an experience, albeit obscure and mysterious, of the One who is beyond our wildest imaginings and more real than anything we have yet known.

This quest for God invites us to return without ceasing to keep fresh that fundamental spiritual intention, so often marginalized by our daily activities or by our suffering and pain. We have to keep coming back to it day after day and to open ever wider to the Presence always and everywhere present to us.

A letter I received from a friend recuperating from surgery in the hospital eloquently witnesses to how this quest brings its own special kind of gifts and repeatedly surprises us.

> Calls come from everywhere, to my phone at home, to the phone in my hospital room, to the homes of friends who relay the message to me. Visits turn into offers to spend hours of time at my bedside. If people come when I am sleeping, they leave a holy card, a copy of a prayer, a letter, flowers, little cards. With beautiful discretion, everything is presence, friendship, a sacrament of God the lover.
>
> I keep feeling that at every level, it is really true that *only love saves*—a love which has become scientific knowledge, study, effort, fatigue, attentiveness, care, and wisdom on the part of the doctors and nurses and chaplain accompanying me. Every one of these visits, no matter how short or fleeting they may have been, became a caress, a connection with me that warmed my life. In this way my hospital room has become a place where silence speaks, sings, and announces the presence of God, where the Holy Spirit is revealed as the Consoler. In ways I never could have imagined, it is a time of grace.

In opening ourselves to the blessing of God at the heart of our fragility and limitations, we become more fully human. Our way of looking at life is transformed little by little and we discover in the ordinariness of daily living so many little reasons for celebrating life. We are pulled by a profound interior movement, an instinct, toward resurrection that casts all the winters of our life in a new light.

We are at the heart of the gospel here. In moments where we may feel abandoned, we live a Good Friday experience of darkness and cold. Then, in what may be a prolonged period of illness, we traverse the silence, anticipation, and waiting of Holy Saturday. But then comes the day when we arise and feel new energy flowing through our veins, and are opened to an intensely spiritual experience of joy. And in this passage we discover the meaning of our baptism: that we are unceasingly passing from death to life.

From this journey with illness, something new is born in us: compassion and solidarity. It is the difficult experiences in our lives that cultivate what is most noble and generous within us. How many men and women, having themselves come through serious illness, have responded by offering their own time and energy in service of those who suffer? Crossing the desert of sickness often results in concrete involvement on behalf of the infirm, whether in the form of intercessory prayer, personal visits, support for the family, or activism for universal health care. This solidarity and compassion is of God. It is literally divine, and it is born from our own experience of neediness and dependence.

Perhaps the most serious and spiritual issue in health care today is the reduction of illness to a technical problem. The issue arises when illness is considered from a purely clinical point of view and the question of meaning is removed from the picture. This technical focus makes it easy for us to forget that *it is the entire person who suffers* an illness. He or she cannot be reduced to a suffering limb or an organ with a limited and localized illness.

When we are companioning someone who is ill, the best way we can offer assistance is by being present, sharing the weakness and powerlessness of the person who is ill, and accepting the terms of the relationship that he or she establishes. It is the patient who is the companion's instructor, and not vice versa. Those who are ill should not be seen simply as people who need assistance. They should also be considered bearers of life's teachings.[4]

The Other Side of the Coin

The late Dr. Elisabeth Kübler-Ross, MD, known for her pioneering work in the field of death and dying, shared some of her personal convictions in an address to her colleagues at a conference of the Association for Holistic Health.

> All the hardships that you face in life, all the tests and tribulations, all the nightmares and all the losses, most people still view as curses, as punishments by God, as something negative. If you would only know that nothing that comes to you is negative. I mean *nothing*. All the trials and tribulations, and the biggest losses that you ever experience, things that make you say, "If I had known about this, I would never have been able to make it through," are gifts to you....
>
> It is an opportunity that you are given to grow. That is the sole purpose of existence on this planet Earth. You will not grow if you just sit in a beautiful flower garden and somebody brings you gorgeous food on a silver platter. But you will grow if you are sick, if you are in pain, if you experience losses, and if you do not put your head in the sand, but take the pain and learn to accept it, not as a curse or a punishment, but as a gift to you with a very, very specific purpose....
>
> Always look at anything that happens in your life from both sides of the coin. There is never just one side to it. You may be terminally ill, you may have a lot of pain, you may not find somebody to talk to about it....Look at the other side of the coin.
>
> You're suddenly one of the few fortunate people who can throw overboard all the "baloney" that you've carried with you. You can go to somebody and say, "I love you," when he can still hear it....Because you know better now that you are here for a very short time, you can finally do things that you really want to do.[5]

Some of my acquaintances have witnessed to "the other side of the coin" in surprising ways. A man who lost his eyesight said, "I have become so aware of things I was not aware of before, that if I was offered my sight back I don't know whether

I would take it." And a mother who lost her young adult daughter in a car accident said two years after her daughter's death: "As painful as it's been, it has brought me to a level of compassion and appreciation for life that is pure gift and that could only have come in this way."

Dr. Kübler-Ross's provocative invitation to look at the other side of the coin may cause us to recoil in protestation, but life will continue to provide us with opportunities to investigate the "hidden blessing" side of things.

Resources for Your Inner Work

A Visualization Exercise[6]

Preparation

Through this visualization you will consider the value and meaning of your life as a whole. Awareness of mortality can bring a perspective, urgency, and richness to the limited precious moments of life, and foster a special care for relationships and priorities. Through a consideration of your mortality, you will enhance your appreciation for the gift of your life.

A guided meditation like this one is a difficult exercise for many in our North American culture because there are not many things that support us in squarely facing realities such as aging and illness and death. The point of this visualization is not to depress you or to trigger a psychological downer. It is offered in the service of life. When you know your treasure is not in infinite supply, what you have is all the more precious.

Tip: Recall a time when you awakened from a nightmare, and how good and grateful you felt to be alive, awake, and well. Remember a time when you have emerged from an ordeal or had a terrible brush with danger, and emerged gratefully, filled with resolve that your life from then on would be different. Take this exercise in that spirit, looking forward to a positive, upbeat outcome.

Exercise

One way of entering into the visualization is by having someone read it to you in a meditative manner, pausing between lines and phrases and giving you sufficient time to enter into it and to become aware of your thoughts and feelings. If you are by yourself, then read the text slowly line by line, stopping where appropriate and closing your eyes so as to better visualize the scene in your imagination. Stay with each scene as long as you feel moved to, continuing with the text as you feel ready. In both instances, allow 25 to 30 minutes.

1. Close your eyes. Take a deep breath and relax. Take a minute to get grounded and centered. Become aware of the weight of your body in the chair...the position of your hands...of your feet upon the floor. Now become aware of your breath...of the air flowing in and out of your nostrils.

2. Imagine that you haven't been feeling at all well recently and you went to the doctor last week for a series of tests. Today is the day you are going to find out the results. It could well be that the tests will reveal a serious illness. See yourself on the way to the doctor's office. Notice what you are feeling.

3. You have reached the office and are sitting in the waiting room. Note the pictures on the wall. What magazines are there to read? Are there other people in the room? Take a good look at them; notice the colors in the room, the rug, the furniture, the lighting. What are you feeling as you wait for your name to be called?

4. Finally your name is called. Be aware of how you feel as you enter the office. See yourself greeting the doctor. Notice the furnishings in the office. Is it bright or dim? Carefully look at the doctor, what the doctor is wearing, the expression on the doctor's face as you are invited to sit down. What kind of person is the doctor?

5. When you ask about the tests, the doctor seems to beat about the bush, to be getting you ready for something. How does this make you feel? You ask the doctor to simply speak to you clearly and frankly and openly. The doctor gives you a long, compassionate look, and proceeds to explain to you that you have an incurable disease. You ask if it is terminal and how long

you have to live. The doctor tells you that you can lead an active life for the next few months, but that the next change of season will likely find you in bed. How do you respond?

6. Notice what you are feeling. Stay with these feelings.... You leave the doctor's office and start toward home. You need some time to be alone with your thoughts. Observe your thoughts as you go along. Notice the other people that you pass by. With this news in your heart, what thoughts come to you about them? What is the weather like, and what effect does this have upon your feelings?

7. You realize that you must decide where you want to go. What do you decide to do? Is there a particular person you'd like to talk to? What are you going to do and whom are you going to see the rest of the day? Consider exactly whom you are going to tell the news to, and whom you will leave in the dark.

8. Consider the lay of the land for the next few months. What are you going to do about work? About vacation? About upcoming important events in your family's life? Are you inclined to change these plans, or to leave things in place? If you opt for changing things, see yourself talking to the people you need to communicate with in order to effect the changes. How do you feel about the next few months?

9. It is three weeks from now. You're at a party. Do people know about your situation? How do you feel being in their company?

10. It's late at night. You go to bed, but you can't sleep. Your thoughts turn to God. What questions would you put to God? What dreams do you have that will have to be revised? What unfinished business in your life will you have to deal with?

11. As you rest in God's presence, what feelings come to you? Can you identify them? Is there fear? What does fear feel like? Is there faith and trust? Go back and forth between the feeling of fear, and the feeling of faith and trust until you get a distinct sense of the difference between the two.

12. Come to rest for a moment in the feeling of faith and trust.

A Testament[7]

Imagine that you have a short time to live. You want to spend some time alone to write down for your friends a sort of testament for which the following points could serve as windows into your life that will enable them to know you better.

1. These things I have loved in life—things I have

   tasted:

   looked at:

   smelled:

   listened to:

   touched:

2. These experiences I have cherished in life:

3. These ideas have brought me liberation:

4. These convictions I have lived by:

5. These are the things I have lived for:

6. These risks I have taken:

7. These sufferings have seasoned me:

8. These lessons life has taught me:

9. These influences have shaped my life [consider persons, occupations, books, events, and so on]:

10. These scripture texts have lit my path:

11. These things I have regretted about my life:

12. These are my life's accomplishments:

13. These are the persons enshrined in my heart:

14. These are my unfulfilled desires:

Prayer

Be at Peace

Do not look forward in fear to the changes in life.
Rather look to them with full hope that as they arise,
God, whose very own you are, will lead you safely
through all things; and when you cannot stand it,
God will carry you in his arms. Do not fear
what may happen tomorrow.
The same everlasting Father who cares for you today
will take care of you then and every day.
He will either shield you from suffering, or will give you
unfailing strength to bear it.
Be at peace and put aside all anxious
thoughts and imaginations.

—*St. Francis de Sales*
(1567–1622)

Surrender

Surrender is a weakness word
in childhood games and
wrestling romps with peers.
But through the years I've come
to see that what it really does
is set you free.

I don't mean here the kind
that comes from fear and poverty;
the letting go I have in mind
requires a sense of safety and security.

While it does pry our fingers
loose from surrogate divinities,
the actual power to surrender is
only given when the heart is tender.

When the inner garden slowly grows
in readiness, the grace is given,
not as something owed, but as
a gift bestowed—almost as though
while we sleep, our hearts breathe deep
and are made ready for letting go.

Chapter Three

Practicing the Little Letting Go's

Renounce and enjoy!
—Mahatma Gandhi

Up until our "golden age," our lives are like a net thrown out ever farther and bringing in an increasingly larger catch. From graduation to first full-time job to marriage and family, growing up is synonymous with accumulating. The accent is upon what we can hang on our walls or in our wardrobe, what we can build or acquire, what we can park in the garage or install in the den.

And after the job titles and the mortgages, the kids' graduations and weddings, the travel abroad and the home redecorating, there is the retirement party. A threshold moment. The turning of a corner. Life becomes simpler. Our needs, fewer.

We are beginning the next phase of our lives. We may continue to enjoy the family home for yet some years, even though half to two-thirds of it stands empty 90 percent of the time. But eventually the size of the yard to keep up and the number of rooms to clean begin to feel like a burden. We experience a growing desire to travel lighter. Our energy is moving more in the direction of the inward rather than the outward journey. We have begun a whole new adventure in life.

When my parents reached this threshold, they decided to downsize and look for living quarters better scaled to their energy levels and needs. In preparation for the eventual move, they spent the better part of a year sorting through all the trunks and boxes in the storeroom; all the envelopes filled with photos in the desk drawers; all the cabinets stacked with little-used plates, cups, and saucers; all the closets laden with clothes covered by plastic dust-protectors.

They took time to remember and to savor the memories of their own and their children's lives: to laugh, to cry, to shake their heads in wonderment. The scouting jamborees. The proms. The baptisms. The family vacations. The athletic teams and class plays and school yearbooks. So many memories, so many blessings, so much richness.

And when they had finished their time of sorting through and setting aside, my father announced in one of his Monday Morning Messages that there would be a family giveaway. He was going to put it all out on the driveway or in the garage, and the children and grandchildren were invited to come and take whatever they could use, from beds and chairs and china to tables and clothing and sporting equipment.

Moving

Feels good
to be throwing out
and giving away.
Files grown thick
over 20 years.
Paper turned yellow.
Books I'll never
read again.
Clothing that's
no longer me.
Wall hangings
to warm a
friend's home now.
Like a boat
listing in the water
heaving off cargo,
my heart comes upright.
Ah! The freedom
of traveling light!

In their letting go, my parents knew that it is what's inside of us that counts, not what's outside. Their value and importance were not tied to the accumulations of their years. In their new, simpler lodgings, they would have the increased freedom to adorn their souls, to refurbish their inner spirits. They had spent many years preparing for the future. Now they wanted simply to enjoy the present.

Letting Go in World Religions

In the story of Siddhartha Gautama, it is the Fourth Messenger who points the way to enlightenment through voluntary renunciation. Practicing the little letting go's enables us to tame our fears of the Big Letting Go and to face it with greater and greater equanimity.

All the religions of the world give an honored place to this theme, even though it is variously named. Hindus, for example, recognize four stages in the life cycle: the student (a time for learning), the householder (a time to apply this education though marriage and child-rearing), the "forest dweller" (a time to step away and reflect on what we have experienced), and the sage (a time to pursue a state of freedom from desire). In this fourth stage, one becomes a sannyasin, a wandering contemplative who consciously seeks to bring about, sooner rather than later, a separation from things to which the rest of us remain attached. Toward this end, the sannyasin eats just one meal a day, doesn't handle money, and abstains from sexual intimacy. All this letting go of potential attachments is a way of preparing for a greater letting go and a propitious rebirth or, better yet, for definitive freedom from the cycle of rebirth and ascendance to the eternal paradise of Brahma.

In Judaism, the story of Abraham, Sarah, and Isaac (Gen 22:1-19) is a cornerstone reference. In the story, Abraham is asked to sacrifice his and Sarah's only son, Isaac. No matter that Sarah had been considered barren and was beyond childbearing age, or that God's covenantal promise to Abraham was to be realized through Isaac. No matter either that Isaac is called upon to sacrifice his own youthful life so full of promise. All three are asked by God to let go—to "die": Abraham and Sarah to their doubts as to whether God knew what God was doing, as well as to their desires to preserve their son's life; and Isaac to his own self-preserving instincts. And in the process, because of their voluntary surrender in trust, Abraham's hand is stayed by the angel, and they are all "reborn" to one another.

In the Christian scriptures, a rich, young man presents himself to Jesus and inquires, "Master, what must I do to gain eternal life?" Jesus recites the commandments to him, and is told by the young man, "I have kept all these from my youth." The Gospel tells us that Jesus then looks upon him with love and says, "Go, sell what you have and give it to the poor, and then come, follow me."

Monasticism and religious life are but two of the ways that this teaching finds expression in Christianity. Those who enter these ways of life vow to live in a manner designed to bring complete inner freedom to pursue these smaller letting go's in order to discover a rich and fulfilling experience of life in growing communion with God.

When Mahatma Gandhi was asked if he could summarize his life in twenty-five words or less, he said, "I can do it in three!" and gave a similar version of Jesus' invitation to the young man: "Renounce and enjoy."

Life's Losses

To freely, consciously embrace smaller letting go's before dying physically is to gradually be reborn in one's inner spirit, fearless in the face of death. Becoming spiritually free does not require becoming a monastic. What is necessary is conscious practice in daily life of little letting go's. Sometimes these letting go's are forced upon us. We perhaps underestimate the role that loss occupies in our lives, and the older we are, the greater is the legacy of loss. Life can be a hard school with a variety of electives, but the lessons we most need are not always easy to find.

Where Is the School?

Holdings of money, looks,
property and position abound,

but where is the school that teaches
holding without owning,
enjoyment without storage,
employment without control?

Where are the mentors
to make clear the difference
between preference and attachment,
desires healthy and disordered?

Who teaches the hard lessons
that no keys are given out
for locking in happiness and peace?
Who offers insightful reflection about
paradoxical moments that satisfy the soul
while simultaneously whetting new desires?

And who's offering a graduate class
or user-friendly online intensive as to
why living with an abiding heartache
is an essential part of being human?

It is important to acknowledge the pain in which our growth is often rooted. Most often, this pain is a result of loss: the loss of a home through bankruptcy or fire; the loss of a spouse through death or divorce; the loss of purpose through unemployment or retirement; the loss of health or mobility through illness or injury; and many other losses, large and small.

Some of them might be actual losses (a significant person, a limb, an important job); others might be symbolic (a loss of identity following the death of a child or a parent); and still others might be termed "disenfranchised losses" because what is lost cannot be socially acknowledged (an extramarital lover), publicly mourned, or socially supported (an elective abortion). There are many ways we could catalog them:

- Material loss of objects, such as keys, money, jewelry
- Relational loss of a person/people by moving, death, divorce

- Functional loss by surgery or the aging process
- Loss of self-image or of hopes, dreams, goals, faith
- Role loss as in job loss or retirement, or loss of accustomed place in the social network

The normal response to these losses is grief. The pain that comes from our losses cannot be quantified or put on a scale because the experience of loss is utterly subjective. The loss of a pet for a preschooler may not feel significantly less hurtful than the loss of personal treasures from a lifetime of toil for a refugee. Places and things that we deeply cherish are invested with meaning far beyond their physical presence. Their loss can find us engaged with a complexity of feelings. But losses like these are also invitations to look deeper, to explore what lies beneath.

On the surface, a house or a ring is just a physical construction or a piece of jewelry. But when they are suffused with memories of people loved and good times shared, of cherished ideals and hopes, they powerfully embody that which is intangible, yet treasured and meaningful. They become almost sacred, and their loss evokes strong emotions that go far beyond their material worth. When we recognize the symbolism behind such places and things, it is easier to understand our struggle with their loss.

When it became necessary for my community to sell one of its properties that was serving as a retreat center, I went to spend a few days there to grieve the loss of it, to say good-bye, to express my gratitude for all the wonderful experiences that were lived both alone and with others in this place of pristine natural beauty: the times of prayer, the walks in the woods, the swims in the lake, the circles of sharing.

And in the course of my days there, it became increasingly clear to me that my feelings around the loss of this place were coming from somewhere deeper. What this woodland sanctuary represented for me was the contemplative dimension of my own spiritual life. In the sanctuary it had provided for reflection and writing, for prayer and rest, it was an ally in rebalancing the active side of my life with the contemplative; an accessible place where a room was always available and the price was always right. Only when I was able to identify this symbolic loss, to recognize that maintaining the inner balance would be even more challenging now, could I proceed to truly letting it go.

When we untangle our feelings of loss and identify the things we actually mourn, we can also see more clearly what we haven't lost. There are other places I can go. None will be as special to me as this one by virtue of all the experiences lived there, but grace is at work in other places, too. We have to let go of the gift we've lost to accept the gift that will next be given.

We walk a tightrope between gratefully receiving material things and creation's spaces and wanting to possess and hold them forever. With each letting go of something or somewhere, we are reminded of their impermanence. The recurrence of loss teaches us to keep our hands open, to adopt a life-giving stance of deeply reverencing things and places, of holding them lightly, of gratefully receiving their blessing, and of relinquishing them when they are taken from us.

The same is true for our relationships. Parenthood has been called a crash course in letting go. There are continuing losses as children, spouses, parents, and friends continue to mature and change over time. The continual evolution of the world around us impacts our relationships. Some we thought would last a lifetime come to an end. As the waves of change break upon the beaches of our lives, even deep relationships we counted upon for the long haul lose their richness and depth and become shallow or strained. We can find ourselves confused, hurt, angry, and alone.

And in all cases, the critical question is: What are the resources we draw upon to face the future?

Through Death to New Life

The recurring motif of Christian faith is that the passageway to new life is an experience of letting go, of loss, of dying. It's called the paschal mystery. *Paschal* comes from the Greek *pasca* and the Hebrew *pesach*, or Passover, referring to the experience of the Israelites passing over from bondage in Egypt to new life as a people in a promised land.

This deep mystery is writ large for us in the events of Jesus' final days. In the liturgical calendar, they are referred to as the Three Great Days: Good Friday, Holy Saturday, and Easter Sunday. And year after year, this mystery is ritually framed once again: new life comes through dying. Death-birth: the principle of all existence.

Death and resurrection are not separate from life. They are not just future. They are present. To look upon the resurrection as a narrow escape from death is to miss the full meaning of human life, to miss the death and resurrection that are present in every moment. It is reflected in the coming and going of the seasons, in the rhythm of our relationships, in the phases of our personal and familial growth.

Did you ever watch children go to school for the first time? Their mothers often leave the school crying. They recognize that the child is dying to that special place the preschooler has within the family in order to live a fuller life. And adolescence literally means an adult is being born, and sometimes in this painful transition, we feel it happening. It happens again when a young person leaves home for college or military service or a faraway job.

When parents return from the airport or the freshman dorm, the house is silent, the room empty, almost as if there had been a death. There has—but a new life full of promise has also begun. One reason for the tears at weddings is because the bride or groom is dying to that special relationship with parents in order to live a new relationship more fully.

Like lovers kissing, death and life touch each other at every moment of our existence. These moments are not to be pushed out of life, are not to be seen as ultimate events but as daily choices, daily rehearsals for our grand finale. These choices are every step of the journey, the inner exodus from the old self to the new. "I die daily," said St. Paul, but he also rose daily. And in this life we rise to new life only by dying, by ceaselessly dying.

Dying to what? On one level, to sin and the pursuit of ephemeral enticements that do not ultimately fulfill. On another level, to simple, legitimate preferences. And on yet another level, to what once was, but no longer is. The only constant is change, so we are always being faced with having to let go.

One illustration of it is seen in our struggle to let go of yesterday, of the past. Not to forget it, just let it go. Whether it's turning fifty, sixty, or seventy. Whether it's losing our health or our hair, our money or our memory, a person we love or a possession we prize.

We Talk About

> We talk about false security
> and issues of control,
> and we think we've learned
> the sacred art of letting go.
>
> Then suddenly life surprises us
> by dropping a boulder on our path,
> and our reaction reveals our truth to us:
> was it one of acceptance or of wrath?

"Little deaths" are letting go of where our security once lay. Whether it's losing family or friends. Whether it's being retired, divorced, or disabled. Whether it's a change of life or a change of pace. We must not cling to what once was but is no more. To try to do so creates suffering.

The universality of this insight is seen not only in the Christian paschal mystery but also in the foundational teaching of Siddhartha Gautama, the Buddha, whose first three Noble Truths are: All life is suffering (everything is transient). The root of suffering is desire (our effort to cling to things that are transient is what causes us pain). The way to reduce our suffering is to reduce our desires (if we stop clinging, it won't hurt as much and we'll become freer to enjoy what is).

In other words, wherever or whatever or with whomever we've been, we dare not cling. We have to move on. And all moving on is a dying, a letting go. In Christian faith, it's the imprint of the paschal mystery on our lives. Only by dying will we rise to fresh life. Only by letting go of yesterday will we open ourselves to tomorrow, where the seeds of fresh life await us.

At one point Gwendolyn, whom we met in the previous chapter, was awaiting medical reports in the months following her chemotherapy treatments to know whether or not the treatments were effective. As Good Friday drew near, she wrote:

> I am reminded of how out of death comes life. This is true in so many aspects of creation and in our personal lives. Facing death has certainly birthed new ways of being, of seeing the world, my life, and everything and everyone in it. It has necessitated enormous grief and "letting go's" as well as new possibilities, opportunities, and plans. Even personally I have changed tremendously through this journey and I know it is far from over. Part of me has died and is in the process of being transformed and resurrected. At times, it is a painful process as well as a joyful one. In spite of the pain, the losses, the grief, the uncertainty, it is a blessed process. I am so very grateful for this wake-up call that is both enabling and creating the necessary changes in my life to make me more authentically who I am. Embracing the uncertainty is part of this process, part of the mystery of life.

Gwendolyn's illness shows how this paschal mystery of new life, which comes through being emptied or letting go of where our security or identity once lay, is revealed in so many aspects of creation. It's as though God has written the message into the natural world all around us so we don't miss it. The acorn carries the tremendous potential within itself of a towering oak tree, but unless its shell cracks open and disintegrates, its full potential will never be realized. The caterpillar crawls into its tomblike chrysalis and metamorphoses into something both in continuity with the old and yet new and more beautiful: a butterfly. From the frozen ground and barren trees of winter, flowers and new leaves burst forth. No dying, no new life. No emptying, no being filled. Everywhere in the universe it is written.

Transitions

Leaf fall, snow fall:
  growth that looks like loss.
Green buds, barkshards, begonias:
  growth that looks like gain.
Seasonal sleight of hand.

Call its bluff—rake the garden leaves
　　for new growth.
There is more than
　　death and endings here.

And in the fallow season
　　when things go slowly
　　or nothing seems to change,
faith is formed from the world
　　of feather and foliage.

Suddenly
　　the eggshell cracks
　　　　the branch blossoms
　　　　　　the bird molts

And the end
　　　　becomes a new
　　　　　　　beginning.

The paschal mystery pertains to human growth and development as well. A child lets go of the security of the womb and enters through the birth canal into a new world. The adolescent lets go of dependency upon grownups to explore the freedom of the teenage years. The teenager relinquishes a cushioned liberty and assumes new risk and responsibility in young adulthood for education, work, and living arrangement. The mature adult with now-grown children faces the new challenges of the retirement years. And the retiree steps forth in faith and trust into old age.

Each stage of the journey offers a new and rich experience of life, but only for those who are willing to embrace the little deaths and to let go of what once was but is no more, opening their hands to the new, fresh experience of life awaiting them. Whenever we are faced in any way with a form of dying or letting go, the paschal mystery of Christ is there to shape our perception of what is happening, and to give an affirming stamp to our hope that out of this "death" will come new life and growth.

German philosopher Arthur Schopenhauer once alluded to how each day is a microcosm of the cycle of birth to death: Each day is a little life; every waking and rising, a little birth; every fresh morning, a little youth; every going to rest and sleep, a little death. Across the whole of our lives, in one form or another, we are dealing with endings, with letting go's, with dyings that, while not the Big Death, range from little to significant experiences of loss. How do we relate to these constant reminders of our mortality? In his book *Responses to 101 Questions on Death and Eternal Life*, Peter Phan describes two alternatives, one very different from the other, which can apply not just to the ultimate end of our life but to our living all along the way.

> In the face of death, one can adopt either of the following two postures. One can run away from it, deny it by trying to achieve immortality through progeny, fame, power. The other posture is to accept, freely and willingly, one's own mortality, with all that this implies in terms of limitation and finitude. Such an acceptance is no mere intellectual assent. Rather it is embodied in a spirituality or way of living marked by gratitude for the gift of life, seriousness about the responsibility of shaping one's destiny through freedom, acceptance of one's limitations and weaknesses, and humble courage in the face of sickness, old age, and death. In this sense, dying is an act the human person performs in freedom, bringing to a definitive end all that he or she has accomplished throughout his or her life.[1]

An Act Engaged with Faith, Hope, Love

When one door closes (death), another door opens (new life). Fixation on the door closing leads to possible depression and despair; trust in another door opening leads to hope. Hope is the healing of the dying. When chemotherapy is over and the pain persists, hope takes over. Death is present in every moment of life; we do not die only once. Death is something we *do*. It is to be *engaged* with faith, hope, and love. If the situation of the dying is hopeless, then the situation of the living is hopeless, too, because dying is a daily part of living. Faith and hope are transcendental virtues when they address what lies beyond our finitude. "Faith is the assurance of things hoped for, the conviction of things not seen" (Heb 11:1). Hope has an object that must be clearly good, is in the future, and is arduous but possible to attain.

Jesus' death was something he actively engaged with in faith, hope, and love. He faced death, his eyes fixed on Jerusalem where he would be handed over to the Romans to be humiliated and killed. When the good-hearted Peter, one of his most trusted disciples, protested that he should never have to suffer such a fate, Jesus rebuked him sternly: "Get behind me, Satan! For you are setting your mind not on divine things but on human things" (Mark 8:33). Through the agony of Gethsemane he came to a profound acceptance of the Father's will: "Am I not to drink the cup that the Father has given me?" (John 18:11). His death was a gift of love he gave to others, an act by which he became part of others' lives. In fact, the ritualization of the way Jesus consciously engaged with his death has become the central act of Christian worship.

> Before he was given up to death, a death he freely accepted, he took bread and gave you thanks. He broke the bread and gave it to his disciples and said, "Take this, all of you, and eat it: this is my body which will be given up for you." When supper was ended, he took the cup. Again he gave you thanks and praise, gave the cup to his disciples and said, "Take this, all of you and drink from it: this is the cup of my blood, the blood of the new and everlasting covenant. It will be shed for you and for all so that sins may be forgiven. Do this in memory of me."[2]

And after this offering is made, the assembly proclaims: "When we eat this bread and drink this cup, *we proclaim your death*, Lord Jesus, until you come in glory" (the emphasis is mine).

When all other alternatives were exhausted, Jesus freely chose the role of the Suffering Servant. Just as his death was the mature outcome of a life lived in freedom, faith, and moral responsibility, so should ours be the culmination of a similar preparation. Death is an *act*: we either willingly accept or definitively rebel against our own utter impotence; it is an act in which we are subject to a mystery that cannot be expressed, the mystery we call God.

Faith: A Tolerance for Ambiguity

There are painful aspects to even a "good death," both for the one dying and for the survivors. There are also deaths that, in spite of all the inner work a dying person has done or might do, are marked by anguish and suffering at the end; final days and hours in which the dying cry out their revolt to God and their feelings of regret at having to leave their loved ones behind. What are we to make of such deaths? Richard Rohr's reflection pertains:

> The great spiritual teachers always balance knowing with not knowing, emphasizing the importance of knowing that you don't know, even your own motives at times. This balancing act became the central biblical great idea called "faith." The recognition that there is a lot we don't know may have been largely lost in our Western culture in our desire to combat secularists, atheists, and unbelievers. The Christian Churches today largely define faith as knowing, and even being certain about our knowing, when actually it means the opposite. Faith is being willing *not* to know, and still being content, because God knows. Faith is a learned "tolerance for ambiguity"—the ability to live with the freedom not to know and not to be right because I no longer use knowledge as power, so I no longer need to be right. I do not even need to know that I am perfectly moral, superior, or good, because I now know as Jesus said, that "God alone is good" (Mark 10:18). Such faith is a gift. It is a gift we can

consciously ask for and grow into, but we do need to know what the goal is.[3]

In the gift of Christian faith, God is more than good. God is love. That conviction drives and sustains faith in the darkest and most tragic of times. It is precisely this conviction that causes us to believe that God rejoices at our ecstasy, grieves at our loss, and empathizes with our suffering. This is the understanding of our relationship with God that coursed through the first sermon of Dr. William Sloane Coffin Jr. after the accidental death of his son whose car went over the edge of a bridge and plunged into Boston Harbor.

The night after his son died, he was sitting in the living room of his sister's house outside of Boston when the front door opened and in came a woman carrying some food for them to eat. When she saw him, she shook her head, then headed for the kitchen, saying sadly over her shoulder, "I just don't understand the will of God."

> Instantly I was up and in hot pursuit, swarming over her. "I'll say you don't, lady!...Do you think it was the will of God that Alex never fixed that lousy windshield wiper of his, that he was probably driving too fast in such a storm, that he probably had had a couple of 'frosties' too many? Do you think it is God's will that there are no street lights along that stretch of road, and no guard rail separating the road and Boston Harbor?"
>
> Nothing infuriates me so as the incapacity of seemingly intelligent people to get it through their heads that God doesn't go around this world with his finger on steering wheels. God is against unnatural deaths. And Christ spent an inordinate amount of time delivering people from paralysis, insanity, leprosy, and muteness.
>
> There are, of course, nature-caused deaths that are untimely and slow and pain-ridden and hard to understand. But violent deaths, such as the one Alex died—to understand those is a piece of cake. As his

younger brother put it simply, standing at the head of the casket at the Boston funeral: "You blew it, buddy. You blew it."

The one thing that should never be said when someone dies is, "It is the will of God." Never do we know enough to say that. My consolation lies in knowing that it was not the will of God that Alex died; that when the waves closed over the sinking car, God's was the first of all our hearts to break.[4]

The spiritual life essentially has to do with an awareness of how important our lives and all that we do are to God. But serenity and trust do not come easily to those whose minds are racked by disease and pain. Dying is often a painful, messy process; we cannot expect to die well in a biological sense. Sometimes the faces of the dying do not show the feelings of acceptance and calm that their loved ones long to see there. Those who continue to radiate faith and love of God through a prolonged period of dying are grace-filled teachers to the rest of the community.

On his deathbed, Plato was asked to summarize his life's work. He replied: "Practice dying." In the 2,300 years since Plato offered this wise admonition, we have developed many ways to "practice living." But what of ways to "practice dying"? In the remainder of this chapter, we will look at two: meditation and what I will call "juggling."

Meditation and Centering Prayer

One way to practice letting go, to regularly interface with our little deaths, is meditation. In the mid-1970s, a Benedictine monk in England, John Main, began to sift through the Christian tradition of contemplative prayer and mine it for the gold of its teaching on a valuable practice that had gone largely underground in the sixteenth century during the Reformation. In 1977, at the invitation of the local bishop, Main founded a small Benedictine community in Montreal, Quebec, and began to teach people how to meditate. This community grew rapidly and became what is today the World Community of Christian Meditation, now based in London, England, and directed by John Main's associate and eventual successor, Father Laurence Freeman.

At the same time, in the United States, another movement, drawing upon the same sources in Christian antiquity and history, was beginning under the leadership of three Trappist monks at Spencer Abbey in Massachusetts: William Menninger, Basil Pennington, and Thomas Keating. Recognizing that *meditation* is a word that means different things to different people, they decided to call this meditative way of praying Centering Prayer.

Meditation, in Western usage, tends to suggest *thinking* and *reflection*, and that is exactly the opposite of its meaning here, so some clarification is necessary. Meditation, in the sense used here, is about reducing the level of activity in the mind as much as possible. It is about *letting go* of thoughts and images and simply coming to rest in God's presence, holding the mind steady and focused on one's sense of that Presence within by means of a sacred word or short phrase (sometimes referred to as a mantra) drawn from the context of one's faith. So it could be a name of God such as Yahweh, Abba, Jesus, Holy Spirit, or a word like *Maranatha* (Aramaic: "Come, Lord").

After coming to a quiet, relaxed position with a straight spine to facilitate breathing and then spending a few moments in focusing the attention on one's breath, one begins to say one's sacred word or phrase very softly in the mind, praying it with faith and with love. Whenever one becomes aware that the mind has been engaged by thought or bodily sensation, one patiently returns to one's mantra, taking it up again.

John Main called meditation "the first death" because in it there is a literal leaving behind of our cherished goods: the analytical intellect that wins us a big salary in the marketplace, the articulate way with words that impresses our colleagues and friends, the lively imagination that is such a rich source of fun and creativity. We leave behind that in which we normally find our security. We seek to become free within from our society's siren call for power, possessions, prestige. The way to enduring spiritual riches is the way of letting go.

Normally, we fly by the radar of education, human effort, personal goals, performance, and production levels. But meditation follows an inner, invisible laser beam, one not based on accomplishments. There is no agenda and nothing to accomplish. Just be before the One Who Is, in full loving attention.

What makes dying hard, of course, is clinging. So in meditation, we let go—of words, images, preoccupations, acquisitiveness. We let go even of the flash of insight, or the idea that promises to resolve a problem we've been working on, that often arises in the middle of our time of meditation. We let go of the feeling or memory that surges up unexpectedly and exercises a strong attraction for us to give it our attention. Letting go of these, our most prized, interior possessions, is truly in its own way an entry into the experience of little deaths.

The letting go is called for as well when I am involved in my normal activities and realize that the time I reserve for meditation has come. In that moment, I am like the man in Jesus' gospel story who has found a treasure in a field or a pearl of great price, and now he must sell everything in order to obtain it. In order for me to be faithful to the rendezvous, I must "sell off" what I am involved in, let go of it in order to retain the pearl of great price: the relationship of intimacy with my Creator, Redeemer, and Sanctifier. This method of prayer is an exercise in letting go of everything.

In a talk on meditation and dying, Father Laurence Freeman put it this way:

> We must prepare for death. Meditation is part of our education.
>
> If meditation were as natural a part of our lives as eating and making love and listening to music, dying would be peaceful.
>
> We are all terminally ill from birth. Somewhere in our DNA is a gene of mortality. Meditation is the way to inner peace because it is a way to the realization of our essential reality as spirit—deathless spirit.

In the Christian vision, the human person is a kind of hologram of God. In meditation we accept the gift of our being as an image of the divine. Meditation isn't concerned with the functioning of mind: analyzing, reflecting, picturing. It is deeper than words.

Neither is meditation concerned with what is particular to the body—movement, sensation, pain, pleasure. Therefore the body is perfectly still during meditation.

In effect, we let go of the two major "screens" on which the concerns of the ego are generally projected: mind and body. We are not rejecting them or pretending that they all of a sudden are not there. Mental distractions and bodily itches continue.

But meditation is concerned with that zone of being called spirit. The sign that we are in the zone is simplicity of consciousness. We enter that simplicity by becoming silent and still. It is not theoretical or investigative, but experiential.

What a person needs to do as they prepare for death is to make peace….Peace is a matter of relationship— with ourselves, others, and God. Meditation is about fulfilling those relationships, about recognizing that we are always and essentially in relationship. Meditation looks like withdrawal because our society has lost the sense of the meaning of the contemplative experience.

The contemplative experience is about *being in the present moment*. If we will enter into the experience, we discover that we are in relationship at a very profound level.

Peace is a reality of the whole person. It's the harmonized totality of the human person. It does not just consist in "peace of mind." It's an energy that cannot be fully explained, that is beyond mind, that is transcendent.

This peace is already within us. That's the starting point of meditation: a basic understanding of the human person that recognizes a transcendent dimension in our being.[5]

Learning to Juggle

I lived in Montreal for twenty-one years, and loved the street life in Old Town Montreal on summer nights and weekends when acrobats, musicians, artists, and dramatists fill the squares. One Saturday afternoon while strolling along, I stopped to enjoy the performance by a pair of jugglers. One of them climbed up and stood on the shoulders of his partner.

Surveying the crowd, he asked if anyone had anything in their shopping bags they could lend him for his juggling act. One person gently tossed him an apple, another a banana, and a third an ear of corn. Then he began launching them into the air in quick succession, all the while balancing himself upon the shoulders of his partner. As we watched his dexterous performance, a question arose in my mind: *Why couldn't we learn to do with our minds what he was doing with his body—to stand atop old, unwanted habits of conditioned thinking and juggle gracefully with anything life tosses us?*

We could start practicing with small things, such as our "likes" and "dislikes." Can I juggle my likes at will? When it benefits someone else, can I turn a dislike into a like? For example, your friend would like to see movie *X* and you would like to see movie *Y*. Or your partner suggests taking a walk, and you're comfy on the couch with your book. Or maybe the friend whom you are meeting for supper expresses an inclination for Greek food, while you had a favorite Italian restaurant in mind.

Can we learn to juggle these likes and dislikes—to stick a bookmark in the middle of the chapter and get up from the sofa to go out for a walk? Or to say, "Well, I had that science-fiction film in mind, but let's go see the comedy you propose"? Chances are, we'll return feeling grateful for having gotten out for a bit of exercise, or for having gone to a movie that made us laugh.

Can we even learn to enjoy doing some things that we dislike, especially when it's in the long-term best interests of either ourselves or others? When we think about it, we realize that people do this all the time. An athlete in training doesn't always feel like rolling out of bed early in the morning, but it's the only time the pool is available for swimming laps, and regular work-outs are necessary for good performance in competition, so he gets up and goes. A mother with a sick child generally doesn't like having her own sleep interrupted throughout the night, but it's in the best interests of her child that she get up and provide comfort or cough syrup, so she does. The friend eating out with someone who is dieting doesn't *have* to forgo dessert, but may freely elect to do so as a gesture of support.

In each case, what is involved is a little letting go of our own preferences and likes, a little act of self-transcendence in which our comfort, convenience, taste, or interest is juggled in order to make room for another's. It's a simple way to broaden the landscape of inner freedom. If I end up going to the movie or restaurant the other had in mind, I can still be happy. My hap-piness is not attached to always getting my own preferences. I can juggle my likes. I can even learn to juggle likes and dislikes.

When we freely choose to spend time with someone whom we don't particularly like, or take a walk with someone whom we positively dislike, we're letting go of our inclinations to walk or talk only with people for whom we feel a positive affinity. At issue is our own inner freedom. When we are bound by rigid tastes in reading, music, movies, food, art, and dress, we end up being a hostage to our own desires. We are not happy unless our own likes are honored. We may as well live in a straitjacket. Learning to juggle removes the jacket and sets us free for a wider range of enjoyment and for the surprise of discovering something new and unexpected: we may end up liking that person with whom we took a walk, or that kind of food we'd never tried before.

When we learn to juggle, to let go of things and preferences before they are taken from us, we are learning to embrace little deaths. And one of the things we learn is that there are new expe-riences of life both before and after each little death. We discover a new kind of joy in the increased freedom, in the ability to find pleasure in new tastes and sounds and sights. We discover to our delight that every little letting go, every little dying to our own ego and its desires, opens into a new and unexpected experience of life.

Juggling, or practicing letting go, is an aware, inward spiritual journey wherein the experience of dying is anticipated in little pieces while one is still alive. Its objectives are a gradual calming of internalized anxieties regarding death, an inner liberation from the fear of physical dying, and the realization of a deathless spirit within. At the heart of it is a teaching found in one form or another in all religions: that the best way to prepare for one's death is to anticipate the death experience in some way while still alive.

Every time we change our ideas and beliefs, it's a letting go of one understanding and the birth of another. Each time a relationship changes or dies and we move on, it's a letting go and a coming alive in a new way. Every time we let go of a preference for a particular seat in the car or plane or for a favorite TV program, it's a little dying, and when we discover some new view or entertainer, it's a little rising.

Each time that happens, our recognition of the paschal mystery imprinted upon life grows, and our trust deepens that what Julian of Norwich wrote is true: "All shall be well, and all shall be well, and all manner of things shall be well." Through this befriending of the little deaths approached in trust and confidence comes a gradual taming of our fears surrounding the Big Letting Go. What is revealed in the befriending is affirmed by the gradual taming of our fears: in death, whether little or big, life is not ended but merely changed.

Resources for Your Inner Work

Reflections

A special place

1. Think of a place that is special to you. Close your eyes and imagine that you are there. Hear the sounds, smell the air, feel the sensations upon your skin. Sit for a while and look around you; savor the scene.

2. Recall the experiences you have lived here, and the people with whom you have shared time here. What are the special moments that come to the fore?
3. Try to discern what draws you here, apart from the attractiveness of the place itself. What does it symbolize for you on a deeper level?
4. Imagine yourself holding it lightly in your hands, and visualize gently letting it go.

A cherished relationship

1. Remember a special relationship you've lost. Conjure up in your imagination the other's image.
2. What did you both appreciate and find difficult about this person?
3. Have you allowed yourself to mourn the loss of the relationship that once was there?
4. Are there any ways in which the relationship continues to be a gift in your life as you move forward?

General reflection questions

1. What letting go's have most profoundly impacted my life?
2. What feelings did I have or do I have as I remember these changes?
3. What did I do, to whom did I go, how did I come to healing?
4. What pain, hurt, anger might I still be carrying?
5. Complete this sentence: Letting go, for me, is like…

Juggling

1. Each day for a week, jot down the various opportunities that present themselves for practicing letting go by juggling your likes and dislikes. At the end of the week, simply as a consciousness-raising exercise for yourself, integrate your various notes and construct a list of them. Reflect on the panoply of opportunities that each day presents for this quiet, discreet spiritual practice.

2. Each week for the next few weeks, choose a few situations from your list in which, if the opportunity arises, you will practice letting go/self-transcendence/spiritual dying.
3. At the end of each day, write down any feelings, observations, or insights you have around your practice, particularly with reference to what you may be clinging to.
4. Over the long haul, ask yourself this question before getting into bed at night: *How did I practice for my death today?*

Meditation

Take a look at two websites replete with resource materials for learning how to meditate:

World Community of Christian Meditation at
    www.wccm.org
Centering Prayer at www.contemplativeoutreach.org

Letting Go

The hardest thing in living
is to receive a grace
a child, a friendship, a fulfilling work
and rejoice in it for the time
it is given
without clinging
without trying to prolong
its visitation.

The pull is so strong
to close around the feeling
the security offered
the identity given
the comfort found;
to lock it up
and possess it,
to freeze the flow
of time and events
saying "Here. Now. Forever!"

But frozen goods
break the teeth.
Better to embrace
the thawed, life-giving moment
in open-hearted thanks,
carrying the gift lightly
in one's hands without grasping,
receiving it as promise and call
to live on the edge of divine desire,
allowing the inner urgent longing
to daily make the blood run
and keep the eyes open and focused,
squinting in the sun towards
the horizon of our Ultimate Hope.

Hang-Gliding in the Alps

Is this what death is like?
One-two-three steps in a body-harness
and all of a sudden the weight of the body
     is *gone*
and you're floating free, like a feather on the wind
with no sense of time, no awareness of heat or cold,
held in a fresh experience of grace, caressed,
gently supported, transported by something invisible,
aware of a wing hovering over you with the sound
of rushing wind, like an ecstatic sigh in your ear,
capable only of looking all around in wonder at familiar things
and seeing all the pieces you've only known up close
in revelatory perspective, in saving relation, one to another,
everything having its place, making its contribution,
filling you with a newfound sense of safety and
setting you free, free as a falcon on the wind.

Chapter Four

The Good Death

*Today a "good death" is generally understood as a
peace-filled acceptance of death where the dying person is
surrounded by and reconciled with loved ones; farewells
have been said; and life tasks completed.*

—Dr. Nuala Kenny

Throughout history, poets, philosophers, and religious teachers
have attempted to make some sense of the eventuality of death.
Poet John Donne wrote that death teaches us about our common humanity. In one of his meditations he wrote: "No man is
an island, entire of itself....Any man's death diminishes me,
because I am involved in mankind, and therefore never send to
know for whom the bell tolls; it tolls for thee."[1]

Death is the cancellation of all our possibilities and activities on earth. It urges us to form coherent, purposeful lives while
we are alive. It encourages us to carefully evaluate our lives and
organize our resources and energies in a useful manner.

During the 1960s, Dr. Elisabeth Kübler-Ross was working
with terminally ill patients in a hospital near Chicago. In her
patient interviews, she noticed what seemed to be certain common states of mind, and she identified the five now-famous
stages that many patients go through in confronting their
deaths.[2] These stages have become popularized and are often
used by those working with the dying as a means of comprehending the experience of those they wish to serve:

1. *Denial:* Subconsciously, we tend to believe that we are immortal and that we will not die. Society and the advertising industry reinforce this attitude, creating the illusion that if we take the right vitamins, exercise regularly, and get enough sunlight and fresh air, we will live forever.
2. *Anger:* In the oft-quoted words of the poet Dylan Thomas, we "rage, rage, against the dying of the light." When faced with the eventuality of our own death, we are likely to pass through a phase of anger, experienced subtly by some and more strongly by others.
3. *Bargaining:* When the anger abates, we often become sly and attempt to bargain with God for more time on earth by promising to change our ways, live more virtuously, undertake a particular work.
4. *Depression:* Eventually, we tire of the struggle, and depression sets in. The loss of energy, mobility, and looks—and various other indignities—may feel like so many hands trying to push us down into a dark hole.
5. *Acceptance:* Finally, we accept our death and peace sets in. Before his death, Pope John XXIII said, "My bags are packed. I'm ready to go."

Not all dying patients follow the same progression, Dr. Kübler-Ross said, but most experience two or more stages; also, these states of mind can be lived in varying sequence. One can come to accept his or her death, and the following day be angry again. "Dying well" should not be seen primarily as something that a dying individual achieves. A serene death is not an accomplishment by which a person must prove his or her spiritual maturity, and a difficult death is not a cause for despair.

The family of the dying lives through these various mind-states too. In addition, Kübler-Ross also observed that people who experience traumatic life changes like divorce or job loss often experience similar stages.

Our Discomfort with Dying

In the Book of Wisdom we read:

> God did not make death,
> and he does not delight in the death of the living...
> for God created us for incorruption,
> and made us in the image of his own eternity,
> but through the devil's envy death entered the world.
>   (Wis 1:13; 2:23–24)

A passage like this helps us understand why we are so much repulsed by death. It is because death is not "natural" for us. As we experience it in the present order of things, it is something extraneous to our nature, fruit of "the devil's envy." Because of this we fight against it with all our might. Our indomitable rejection of death is the best proof that we are not made for it, and that it does not have the last word. The Book of Wisdom later assures us that "the souls of the righteous are in the hands of God, / and no torment will ever touch them" (3:1).

Fear of death is written deeply into every human being. All of humanity cries out: "I do not want to die!" We try not to think about it and, when we do, it is easier for us to grant that it exists for others rather than for ourselves. But the thought of death does not allow itself to be put aside so easily. So all we can do is repress it or play down its seriousness. As for aging and illness, we never cease to look for remedies, which are really remedies for death. One of these is called offspring: surviving through one's children. Another is fame. In our day, a new pseudo-remedy is spreading: the doctrine of reincarnation.[3]

This doctrine is found in the most varied religions in different forms. In all these religions and schools of philosophy, the theory of reincarnation was only one theory among others. In India (Hinduism and Buddhism), it became a dogma pervading the entire religion and the totality of its thought. There is a fundamental difference, however, between the historic theories of reincarnation (Hindu) or transfer of karmic energy (Buddhist) and the modern Western ones. In Hinduism, the cycle of rebirth is a fearful thing, something people want to be liberated from. The wheel of rebirth is tied to notions of guilt and punishment, and it evokes fright.

By contrast, in Western thought, reincarnation represents a new and positive opportunity. Here, reincarnation is not a burden, but rather a comfort positively associated with new possibilities for self-fulfillment. Recent surveys by the Barna Group, a Christian research nonprofit, have found that a quarter of U.S. Christians embrace reincarnation as their favored end-of-life view.[4] Scriptural and doctrinal difficulties aside, could this be but another expression of our fear of death and our tendency to deny it? The data implies that persons of faith experience the same difficulties as others in acknowledging the limits of medicine to cure. But acknowledging death can offer a precious time of grace, reconciliation, and healing.

Palliative (from the Latin word meaning "to cloak or to shield") care is an approach that emphasizes pain relief, symptom control, and spiritual and emotional care for the dying and their families, rather than an effort to cure the underlying disease. While we view life and health as gifts from God, they are not absolute values that force natural life to be preserved at any cost when it merely prolongs the dying process and becomes burdensome on the patient. Dr. Nuala Kenny, policy adviser to the Catholic Health Alliance of Canada, describes a "good death" as a peaceful acceptance of death where the dying person is surrounded by, and reconciled with, loved ones—where the farewells have been said and life tasks completed. It is not a frantic and fearful pursuit of a saving technology to the last breath, nor has it anything to do with assisted suicide and euthanasia. An intentional shift to the notion of palliative care resonates with the Christian notion of the good death.

Palliative care neither hastens nor prolongs dying. It uses medicine to alleviate pain and control symptoms, and it respects the dying person's values and life goals while providing support. Palliative care resonates strongly with Catholic social justice teaching on human dignity, social interdependence, solidarity, subsidiarity in decision making, the preferential option for the poor—especially those who are poor in health—and an understanding of the common good. Palliative care, in short, is a holistic response to the questions that may often trouble those who have reached the final stage of their lives. It represents a fully human response to the suffering of body, spirit, and soul.

In an article entitled "Will We Ever Arrive at the Good Death?" in *The New York Times Magazine*, Robin Marantz Henig reflects on how our deep discomfort with dying is not only reflected in our medical system but in the evolution in palliative and hospice care as well, two movements that took root and grew in the 1960s and 70s and are widely appreciated today.[5]

Palliative medicine is a kind of pre-hospice care, extended at the first diagnosis of a terminal illness. It's a branch of medicine that takes as its mission the prevention and relief of suffering, in particular the suffering associated with terminal illness. The concept of hospice originated in Great Britain where Dame Cicely Saunders, a social worker turned physician, opened the world's first modern hospice, St. Christopher's, in 1967. The first American hospice, built on the St. Christopher model, opened in Connecticut in 1974 with financing from the National Cancer Institute. From then, the movement grew, led by a handful of nurses and a slightly larger number of volunteers.

As a home-based health-care service, hospice began as an antiestablishment, largely volunteer movement advocating a gentle death as an alternative to the "medicalized" death many people had come to dread. Most people want to die naturally and at home. But in recent years, Henig observes, hospice itself has become institutionalized, and it no longer means quite what most people take it to mean. Today there are hospice patients on ventilators or with feeding tubes, or who are getting pacemakers or receiving blood transfusions and cardiopulmonary resuscitation. It's all part of the new trend in hospice toward "open access," meaning that terminally ill patients can continue chemotherapy and other treatments.

With hospice expanding its range of services and with palliative care becoming a new medical subspecialty, the natural, machine-free deaths we say we want are starting to look a lot like the medicalized deaths they were meant to replace. In its own way, our health-care system reflects our deep ambivalence about dying.

Though our newspapers and broadcasts present us with daily accounts of death in the form of murders, suicides, abortions, assassinations, vehicle crashes, and acts of terrorism and war, death generally comes for most of us with unpredictable timing from predictably fatal chronic disease. But since the diseases are predictably fatal, why do we so often feel blindsided by death, even the death of an elderly person suffering from a long-term condition? Because the hardest thing to do is to really, deeply believe that we or our loved ones will die. We choose not to think about it. We pretend that it does not exist, or that it exists only for others, but not for ourselves.

Another example of our ambivalence about death is our unwillingness to look it straight in the face even as we make noises about accepting it. The words we use as euphemisms belie the resistance within: it's a "final curtain" or "passing on" or "leaving the body."

According to the National Hospice Foundation, one-quarter of American adults over forty-five say they would be unwilling to talk to their parents about their parents' death—even if their parents had been told they had less than six months to live. Half of all Americans say they are counting on friends and family members to carry out their wishes about how they want to die, but 75 percent of them have never spelled out their wishes to anyone. It's a good bet that a significant subset of that 75 percent have never faced the questions involved and come to some decisions for themselves. The Inner Work Resources at the end of this chapter will provide you with the opportunity to engage with some of those questions.

None of us, of course, can say what it's really like to die. We only get one chance at it, and there's no reporting back from the field, near-death experiences notwithstanding. In their book *Handbook for Mortals*, Joan Harrold, Joanne Lynn, and Janice Lynch Schuster write about a seriously ill patient who opens his eyes and sees a nurse. "Am I dead yet?" he asks. "No," says the nurse. He thinks for a moment and then says, "How will I know?" Studying death is akin to examining a black hole: there's something intrinsic to the very process that defies our ability to analyze it.[6]

The Good Death

I grew up with the Beatles. George Harrison seemed to be the one who provided the spiritual impetus of the band. He was the one who fell for the Maharishi, took the sitar lessons, and gave the most time and depth of thought to Indian mysticism. He was a seeker who knew that religion engaged you at a deeper level. This openness to something bigger than the vanity of celebrity surely contributed to why he wrote great love songs, not about possession or passion but about sidelong glimpses of transcendence, the "something in the way she moves." Spiritual wonder pervaded his best work, "Here Comes the Sun" and "My Sweet Lord," with the otherworldly jangle of India providing the background.

The statement released by his wife Olivia and son Dhani after he died only confirmed these perceptions. They used his own phrases, like "Everything else can wait, but the search for God cannot wait," "Love one another," or the remark that he was "just going on to another place." But it was the description of his actual death that remained glued to the wall of the mind. They said simply, "He left this world as he lived in it, conscious of God, fearless of death, and at peace."[7]

Conscious of God, fearless of death…

If you had a religious upbringing, the words might take you back to what my Irish ancestors called the good death. "Oh, she had a beautiful death, now!" they would say.

Pauline's Story

My cousin Pauline, a flight attendant for Northwest Airlines, health conscious and superfit in her late forties, discovered while showering one Sunday a lump in her breast. On Monday she went to the doctor for X-rays. On Tuesday she had a biopsy taken. On Wednesday she learned it was malignant. On Thursday she scheduled surgery. Life can change fast! We can never sit back and say with finality, "I have good health!" because our bodies are constantly changing. Wellness is a matter of being attuned to how we are and working constructively with the truth of the situation.

After her surgery, Pauline sent an e-mail around to family members. "I've never been happier in my life," she said. "I love my new home. I have a good network of friends developing. I feel very physically fit. Tell the family not to push the panic button because I'm not. I may have cancer in my body, but they will remove it, and overall I am *well*." And she was, in the true sense of that word: she was attuned to her situation, facing it with hope and a positive attitude, and working constructively with it.

Befitting her long career as a flight attendant, Pauline lived out of a "journey spirituality." "Life is a journey," she would often say, "and we've all got lessons to learn." And Pauline was always ready to share with you the lessons she was learning. She had strong convictions about things, especially where health was concerned. Her cancer was diagnosed in August, and for three and a half months she resisted taking the recommended medical treatment and sought healing in the most holistic and least invasive way possible. When it became clear that it was not working, she altered her course. But by that time, it was too late. Three months later, in November, another nodule was discovered. It, too, proved to be malignant. A CAT scan now revealed cancer in her spine, pelvis, and legs. The doctors told her she had about six months to live.

She never said, "Woe is me!" Simply: "Life's a journey and we've all got lessons to learn." And she set about learning the lessons that having cancer could teach her.

Her decision to have her head shaved as she began chemo treatments was so characteristic of her open and proactive approach in playing the cards that life dealt her. And as her treatment progressed, she just became more grounded and centered in what really matters. "All my barriers are down," she would exclaim with a laugh. "It's just me—I don't even have any eyebrows left!"

And rather than withdrawing into seclusion and cutting everyone off, she sent out a remarkable card at Easter time presenting herself bald and looking right at you. On the inside, just to make sure you didn't miss the lesson, were the words: "Surrender. Embrace. Peace."

As her brother Wally noted, while some of her outer beauty was compromised by her disease, her inner beauty shined even brighter.

She was our teacher. She never went beyond the first year of college, but she taught us some important lessons about living, and she taught us how to die. She taught us to work the balance between solitude and community, between time alone and time with friends and family. She taught us to take good care of our bodies, to eat nourishing food, to exercise regularly, to read books that feed the soul, and to take advantage of the opportunities afforded by travel—all for a better quality of life, as long as the gift is given to us.

But most of all, she taught us the courage and strength that faith in the resurrection provides as she faced her death. She participated in a funeral workshop at her parish, and in a program for the terminally ill called Pathways. She talked openly and freely about her death. She was serene and comfortable about where she was going. Death is real, and it is not to be feared if we have done our inner work. Pauline did her inner work.

And what a death she lived! In her final weeks, her brother Wally and his wife Denise and their two daughters took her into their home. On June 27, when it appeared that she could go at any moment, a priest was called in to anoint her, and the family gathered around her bed and laid hands on her in prayer.

Pauline revived the next day, and within twenty-four hours the family organized a birthday party for her in the spirit of *Tuesdays with Morrie*—bringing all the friends and family together not *after* her death, but *before* it when she could enjoy them. The back lawn was adorned with round tables and floating candles. "We love you" balloons were waving in the air against a sunset over the lake. She was miraculously given the energy to be up and about, circulating with the seventy-five guests and taking time to talk with each one.

Wally and his family will tell you: having Pauline in their home during the last three weeks of her life was a blessing for them and for her. They were able to spend whole days together. Denise told her, "I'm finding out so much more about you in these few weeks than in our whole previous lives." They would start the day with a reading from scripture, enjoy quality conversation at intervals throughout the day, and end their days in prayer.

The night before Pauline died, on July 4, there were, appropriately, fireworks over the lake, and her two nieces gave her a long foot and hand massage. Passing by her room on his way to bed, Wally saw her lying in bed, reaching up to the ceiling with both arms outstretched, and heard her say, "Let's go." And then, as though she was seeing something on the other side, she sighed, "It's absolutely perfect!"

The next morning, those taking turns keeping vigil with her during the night—her mother, brothers, and nieces—were all gathered around her bed when she took her last breath. Wally looked at the clock. It was 6:26 a.m., the exact time of the day on which she was born forty-nine years earlier. It was, as Denise recounted, "as peaceful and beautiful as death could be."

The sickness that brought Pauline face-to-face with her finitude was a time of rich blessing in her life. At her funeral, a line from one of the readings summed it up: "Christ will be exalted now as always in my body, whether by life or by death" (Phil 1:20).

The Difference Faith Makes

In his audio series on "Wisdom from the Celtic World," the Irish priest-poet-philosopher John O'Donohue relates a story about a young mother of twenty-seven with two children, five and three, who was five months pregnant with a third and who was very sick with leukemia. When he arrived in the hospital room on this particular night, she was hooked up to various machines and had an oxygen mask on. "Am I going to die?" she asked him. He told her he didn't know, but he would find out and tell her what was happening. So he left the room in search of the doctor who was on duty for the night and asked him what the situation was.

> "She's dying...she'll be dead before ten o'clock in the morning."
> ...So I went in then...and sat down with her and took her hand in mine and told her that she was going

to die soon....She went into total panic and was frozen and petrified with fear.

...I prayed harder than I ever prayed that I would get the words that would make a little bridge for her and enable her to make the journey. I knew her life very deeply and I started to bring up all the memories for her. I told her of her own goodness and beauty and kindness. She was a woman who...was always trying to do good for people. She acknowledged it and I told her then that there was no need for her to be afraid in any way. That she was going home and that there would be a welcome for her and that God who had sent her here to the earth for this time would welcome her and embrace her and take her so gently and lovingly home.

...Little by little this incredible serenity and calmness came totally over her and all of her panic was transfigured into a kind of serenity that I have rarely met in the world. Every bit of anxiety and worry and fear had completely vanished and she was totally in rhythm with herself, attuned and completely still.

"Now you have to do the most difficult thing you have ever done in your life," I told her. "You have to say good-bye to each member of your family...." I went out and rounded up each member in the corridor and told them that each one could go in for five or ten minutes...and tell her how much they loved her and what she meant to them....

Each one brought her the gift of acknowledgement and recognition and love. Then I went in to see her and I anointed her with holy oil and we all said the prayers together. She was wheeled out of the room smiling and serene and went on the journey that she had to make alone.

It was an incredible privilege for me to be there and to be able to accompany her, and it taught me something. It completely broke for the first time my own fear of death. It showed me that if you live in the world with kindness and don't add to other people's burdens but try to serve love, then when the time comes for you to make the journey, you will receive a serenity and peace and a beautiful kind of welcoming freedom that will enable you to go to the other world with great elegance, grace and acceptance.[8]

The man who shared that story, John O'Donohue, once wrote that "endings seem to lie in wait." His certainly did. He died in his sleep at fifty-two while on vacation in France. And the way his friend in that hospital room faced her death was a gift to him.

A Grace-Filled Teacher

When Joseph Bernardin, the cardinal archbishop of Chicago, died in 1996, *Newsweek* magazine featured his peaceful face on its cover with the headline: "Teaching Us How to Die."[9] Can you think of any other occasion when you have seen someone in a clerical collar—besides the pope—on the cover of a national newsmagazine? If you can't, take that as a measure of the importance of his "teaching."

At thirty-eight, Bernardin became the youngest Catholic bishop in the United States. He had a gift for administration and was named the first general secretary of the National Conference of Catholic Bishops, created in 1967 after the Second Vatican Council. Five years later he was appointed archbishop of Cincinnati, and two years after that was elected to head the American Catholic hierarchy and became a key player of the World Synod of Bishops in Rome. In 1982, he was appointed archbishop of Chicago and within the same year was named a cardinal. In the fourteen years that followed, he continued to shape the public face of American Catholicism, defining for Catholics the "seamless garment" ethic, which united Church opposition to abortion, euthanasia, capital punishment, poverty, and the nuclear arms race in a "consistent ethic of life."

At sixty-seven, he learned he had cancer of the pancreas. And just when he thought that surgery had put him out of danger, an examination confirmed that resurgent cancer cells were now destroying his liver. This time there would be no reprieve. He could see all the way to the end of his life, and he knew the end was near.

He was given the kind of end we all might wish for: three months to sign off on tasks undertaken, to ask for forgiveness, to say good-bye. On the very day he learned his cancer was terminal, he made a public promise to use whatever time was left in a way that would be of benefit to those he had been called to serve. There were, he felt, lessons of faith yet to be learned and lessons of dying yet to be taught. The churchman who had always been confident of his control had to learn to let go, to surrender. That, too, was a lesson he passed on to others. A public man, he chose to die a public death. In the words of a rabbi friend of his, "He was inside with his outside, outside with his inside, which is rare."[10] He faced his death as openly and publicly as he had faced the issue of abuse in his archdiocese and also the false accusation of abuse made against him personally, which took its toll even though the accuser himself later admitted he had lied.

In a handwritten note, Bernardin bade farewell to his fellow bishops, who were meeting in Washington, DC, asking them for their prayers "that God will give me the grace and strength I need each day." He sent an early Christmas card to his priests and friends and squeezed the hand of those who came to say good-bye. One of his last acts was to sign off on the manuscript of his book *The Gift of Peace*, in which he discussed his preparations for death.

A feeling of helplessness came over me in the doctor's office....Remembering that moment now, I think of God and his plan for me. I think of others, too, who sit in a state of absolute anxiety as they wait to hear from doctors what their fate will be. I now realize that when I asked my doctor for the test results, I had to let go of everything. Again. God was teaching me just how little control we have and how important it is to trust in him. I needed God at that moment, as I had needed him before....

One of the things I have noticed about illness is that it draws you inside yourself. When we are ill, we tend to focus on our own pain and suffering. We may feel sorry for ourselves or become depressed. But by focusing on Jesus' message—that through suffering we empty ourselves and are filled with God's grace and love—we can begin to think of other people and their needs; we become eager to walk with them in their suffering and trials....

My decision to discuss my cancer openly and honestly has sent a message that when we are ill, we need not close in on ourselves, or remove ourselves from others. Instead, it is in these times when we need people the most.

I have tried to live my life openly and honestly with a deep commitment to the Lord, the Church, and the human community...to put my faith into action, to live out the principles that guide my life.[11]

And live them out he did. Upon learning that he had cancer, he began to build a parish without walls, boundaries, or doctrinal lines, starting with fellow patients at the cancer clinic, which is now named after him. When coming for his own chemotherapy treatments, he never left without visiting and encouraging all the other patients, following up with phone calls, letters, and special visits at crucial moments, delegating his administrative duties as archbishop to his staff. He also made time to visit parishes to anoint the sick and on one occasion consoled a prisoner about to be executed, observing that they both had a sentence of death.

He was engaging in the remedy that always works. There are very few remedies in human experience that always work. But there is one remedy that, whether in the case of great sorrow or disappointment or times in which life simply doesn't make any sense, works infallibly so long as it is carefully and consistently applied: Get out of yourself and help someone else. Generosity, mercy, courtesy, concern for others are all ways of fulfilling the counsel of Jesus to love your neighbor as yourself and to be merciful as God is merciful.[12]

Dr. Ira Byock, president of the American Academy of Hospice Physicians, writes in his book *Dying Well* that good deaths can be fostered by helping patients repair relationships, respecting the patient's integrity, helping the dying to live as fully as possible, reducing their pain, and allowing time and space for transcendence and for letting go.[13]

But there's no getting around it: the best preparation for a good death is a good life. The work of dying well is, in large part, the work of living well.

Lessons for Our Living

There are several lessons to be learned from reading even a few excerpts of Cardinal Bernardin's life: We're never done growing. Remember the importance of honesty and transparency. Adhere to our beliefs, and trust in God. But one lesson we should not miss, says Father Ronald Rolheiser, is this:

> Anything we do to prepare for death should not be morbid or be something that distances or separates us from life and each other. We don't prepare for death by withdrawing from life. The opposite is true. What prepares us for death, anoints us for it, in Christ's phrase, is a deeper, more intimate, fuller entry into life. We get ready for death by beginning to live our lives as we should have been living them all along. How do we do that?
>
> [Theologian] John Shea once suggested that the kingdom of heaven is open to all who are willing to sit down with all. That's a one-line caption for discipleship. In essence, the single condition for going to heaven is to have the kind of heart and the kind of openness that makes it possible for us to sit down with absolutely anyone and to share life and a table with him or her. If that is true, then the best way we can prepare to die is to begin to stretch our hearts to

love ever wider and wider, to begin to love in a way that takes us beyond the natural narrowness and discrimination that exists within our hearts because of temperament, wound, timidity, ignorance, selfishness, race, gender, religion, circumstance, and our place in history.

We prepare to die by pushing ourselves to love less narrowly. In that sense, readying ourselves for death is really an ever-widening entry into life.[14]

In his last work before he died, Henri Nouwen spoke of how the final task in life is to give one's death to others.

Yes, there is such a thing as a good death. We ourselves are responsible for the way we die. We have to choose between clinging to life in such a way that death becomes nothing but a failure, or letting go of life in freedom so that even our death can be given to others as a source of hope. This is a crucial choice and we have to "work" on that choice every day of our lives. Death does not have to be our final failure, our final defeat in the struggle of our life, our unavoidable fate. If our deepest human desire is, indeed, to give ourselves to others, then we can make our death into a final gift. It is so wonderful to see how fruitful death is when it is a free gift.[15]

This is a gift, a teaching, that is not transmitted simply at the end of life, but all along the way as we demonstrate how to live with faith and serenity the "little deaths" that mark our journey through life. Rolheiser also addresses this idea of the gift that our death can be:

When someone we know dies, we are left with a feeling, a tone, a color, something in the air, of either guilt or blessing. The feeling isn't based so much upon whether the person died accidently or naturally, was young or old, or whether or not we were present to him or her at the time of death. It takes root rather in how that person lived and how he or she related to life in general, more so than how he or she related specifically to us. That's part of the mystery of death. It releases a spirit.

Before he died, Jesus told his disciples that it was only after he was gone that they would be able to grasp what he really meant for them. That is true for everyone. Only after we have died will our spirits fully reveal themselves. And this works in two ways: If our spirits have been loving, death will reveal our real beauty (which, in this life, is always limited by wounds and shortcomings). Conversely, if our spirits, at the core, have been petty and bitter, our deaths will also reveal that. The death of a generous, gracious soul releases blessing and makes others feel free, just as the death of a bitter, clinging soul pours out accusation and makes others feel guilty.

How can I make my death a gift for others? By the way I live.[16]

If we live with graciousness and forgiveness, then our death will mean new freedom and courage for those who knew us. They will be able to take the next step in their living with less fear and guilt. The way we die will become an important part of the way they live.

Radical Discipleship

The Gospels, the mystics, and the great spiritual writers concur that there are three discernible stages to the spiritual journey. They express it in various ways and do not all use the same words, but the idea of three levels of discipleship is there.

The first level, which might aptly be termed Essential Discipleship, is the struggle to get our lives together, to achieve basic human maturity...to develop the capacity to put others before ourselves. The second level can be called Generative Discipleship and is the struggle to give our lives away in love, service, and prayer. And the third level can be called Radical Discipleship and consists in the struggle to give our deaths away, that is, to leave this earth in such a way that our deaths themselves become our final gift and blessing to our families, churches, and society.[17]

Let me share with you two stories of radical discipleship.

On a Labor Day weekend, my mother let family members know that Dad was experiencing swelling in his right leg and foot and that a doctor in town had told her "it might be a blood clot" and he should have it looked at. A subsequent CAT scan revealed swollen lymph glands, and a few days later a biopsy indicated that it was an aggressive cancer. A later PET scan revealed that the cancer had spread throughout the lymphatic system and on October 9 the doctor told him he had "months" to live.

Dad elected to go with ten treatments of radiotherapy to treat the swollen lymph glands in the groin area in the hopes that it would stop their constant secretion of fluids with resultant painful swelling of the legs and feet. But the treatments had debilitating side effects that weakened him drastically and taxed his system. Suddenly the doctors who two weeks ago were saying he had "months" to live—six months, eight, twelve? We were still in the process of absorbing that shock—were now saying it might be "days," with the radiology oncologist saying possibly the next twenty-four hours.

The immediate family members were suddenly packing their bags for an unexpected gathering. By nightfall, we were all in the hospital room: my sister from the West Coast and me from the East, one brother from Ohio and two others in Minnesota.

Dad was starting to wake up from the medications administered earlier in the day and beginning to take cognizance of the fact that all his children were gathered in the room. A background to life and family gatherings in our home is music. Dad and Mom sang in choirs all their lives, so it wasn't long before we started to celebrate our being all together with song—campfire songs, Scout songs, Broadway hits, church hymns, pop favorites. It went on for two and a half hours. The nurse said she would put her ear to the door every time she passed by to hear what we were singing now. Dad hummed along with some, hoarsely sang a few verses to others, and occasionally put out a special request. At one point he looked around the room and said, "Thank you, Lord, for this wonderful gathering! Since you're all here, I just gotta tell you that you're a great group!" All our lives he had affirmed us, and was doing so even now in his last hours as a final gift.

About 11 p.m., Dad was fading back into sleep after a lively evening. One of my brothers spent the night with him, climbing onto his bed and rubbing his back in the early morning, relating afterward, "It also gave me an opportunity to express my tears."

At 9 a.m. the next morning, we were all in the room for a bedside liturgy. It was November 1, All Saints Day. We celebrated the Eucharist and I anointed him, inviting all the family to lay hands on him in blessing, one after the other. "Dad, you've received the anointing of the sick and holy communion. We're all here around you and love you very much," we said. "We'll take good care of Mom. You can let go whenever you feel ready." And from the bed came a whispered "Amen."

In the course of the day we chanted the Litany of the Saints around his bed, sat quietly in meditation, and prayed the rosary, each of us leading a decade. The closing line of the Hail Mary— "Pray for us sinners now and at the hour of our death"—never seemed more appropriate as a prayer.

Evening came, and with it more songs, on a lighter note this time, from *Camelot* and the *Sound of Music*. One of my brothers came up with the idea of getting some ice cream and passing it around in honor of Dad's custom of "leveling it off." It was a little ritual for which my father had become famous in the family. Often before going to bed at night, with a long-handled spoon for deep dips and a little hand towel neatly draped over his shoulder for wiping off the excess on the knuckles and around the lips, he would proceed to enjoy his favorite food, always leveling it off before closing the container.

Within the hour we had a half gallon of cookies 'n cream in the room. The nurse, who had heard me recount Dad's little ritual the night before, brought in a half dozen hand towels and spoons, one for each of us to throw over our shoulder as we dug into the ice cream.

Before we had emptied our bowls, we noticed that Dad's breathing pattern had changed and was becoming more pronounced, with longer spans between each breath. We put down the ice cream and moved in close to him, stroking his hands and arms, face and head; all of us watching his breath, aware that this was the end, that each breath we were witnessing could be the last one. And within ten minutes, it came: a long, heavy exhalation that was not followed by an inhalation. He simply stopped breathing. It happened so peacefully, without a shudder or a cry or any movement of the body. Just a breath that was not followed by another. I moved my fingers to his neck pulse and felt nothing. There we were, his wife and children, close to him and to one another, our hands caressing him, stroking his skin...and now this man who had given us life was lifeless.

The moment was surreal for us all. We simply sat there, absorbing what had just happened, shedding tears, telling one another that our prayers had been answered, expressing gratitude that he would know no more suffering, that God had taken him so peaceably and quickly, and on All Saints Day.

Transforming Elements: Faith, Family, Friends

The second story of radical discipleship is how my mother faced her own death.

Within a few months after my father's death, my mother announced to the family that at eighty-seven her new ministry was to visit the sick and bury the dead. She rejoined the funeral choir and proceeded to make regular visits to friends in healthcare centers.

About a year later, in a phone conversation on the first day of February, she shared how she had sung in the choir that morning and how, while picking up her glass of water while attending a Serra Club luncheon at noontime, she noticed a lack of sensation in her fingers. She related how, that afternoon, in going for her winter indoor walk in a large local mall, she had to stop and rest three times because her legs "just didn't have the strength they normally do."

In the course of the conversation, she told me about the eighty-four-year-old at whose funeral she had sung that morning, and commented, "People are dying all around me. I could go any day, too." To myself I thought, "Oh come on, Mom—you're going to live for another ten years just like your mother" (who lived to be ninety-nine).

The next morning, a Tuesday, when the numbness recurred in both hands and feet, she called her doctor to make an appointment for a checkup. The office nurse informed her that her doctor had just retired and that it would be some weeks yet before his replacement would arrive. She suggested Mom go to urgent care at the local hospital and have a few tests taken, which she did that very afternoon. The intake nurse was somewhat incredulous that the only "medication" my mother was on was a calcium pill, a multivitamin, and eye drops.

The tests revealed that all her blood counts—red cell, white cell, platelets—were 50 percent to 80 percent below normal. When the physician came back into the room, he surprised her by saying that he wanted to keep her in the hospital overnight and run more tests the next day.

By Thursday, the specialist treating her in the hospital told one of my brothers that he believed her bone marrow had ceased manufacturing blood, most likely due to a disease process in the bone marrow itself. He had sent a bone marrow biopsy off to the Mayo clinic for analysis. On Friday he was back in her room with the results and told her that she had acute leukemia. "How long do I have?" she asked. "Normally," he said, "about two to three months."

Again, the family was stunned. Again, the whole thing seemed surreal. In the following week, Mom opted in favor of hospice care so as to be able to spend her remaining time in the comfort and familiarity of her home. If she were to develop an infection, fever, bleeding of any kind, there would be no need to go to a doctor or an emergency room or even to call 911. "Simply call hospice," they said, and they would come to us, contact the doctor, give us coaching on what to do, and manage all the fees through Medicare. Their primary focus was her comfort while the disease played itself out, rather than trying to extend her time with life-support measures. With conference calls and e-mails, we quickly organized our calendars to take turns keeping her company in the coming months.

She continued to be in good spirits and very much at peace, exclaiming that she herself couldn't believe this was happening. When a daughter-in-law brought over a chicken casserole, she commented on how good the dish was and that she should get the recipe, but then humorously reflected how she probably wouldn't have time to make it anyway. When something came up like bill payments and required her attention, she'd laugh and say, "Isn't it great! I won't have to worry about that much longer!" When we told her at one point that we all just thought she would go on forever, she laughed and said, "I want to keep on going, but if I can't, I just want to go!"

Valentine's Day fell on a weekend, and all the children and grandchildren and great-grandchildren who were able gathered in her home. We sat around the table, talking with her about her illness. Then we prepared the table for a family Eucharist. The Gospel for the day appropriately featured Jesus in the boat calming the storm on the lake. Mom gave a powerful testimony of how she wasn't afraid, and felt close to Jesus and the Father, to Mary and Joseph; how her relationship with each had been nurtured over the years through prayer, which, she reminded us, "requires time and commitment." I anointed her with the oil for the sick and we all laid hands on her in prayer. At the end of Mass, I presented her with an honorary doctor of divinity degree, "certified" with the signature of all the family "trustees" (her children), that I had made up for her in recognition of her "Life-long Dissertation on Availability for Service in Love."

The following day, after the others had gone, the two of us sat and planned her wake and funeral, choosing readings and songs, pallbearers, readers, and eucharistic ministers. The next evening we enjoyed a candlelight-and-wine, two-hour dining experience while sharing memories and stories. Around nine in the evening, she suggested we do our final piece of work—a draft of her obituary. We thought doing it over a banana split would help the process, so with the obituaries from that day's newspaper in one hand for formatting reference and a banana split liberally doused with chocolate sauce in the other, she proceeded to talk me through it.

"I feel so blessed," she said. "God has given me two to three months' notice to get my affairs in order and to enjoy some quality time with family and friends." And in the ensuing weeks she set about going through all the closets and drawers, giving clothing to local charities and thrift stores, and placed on the table a large notebook containing an inventory of all the furniture, pictures on the walls, dishes, silverware, glasses—everything that might be of interest to another family member—inviting each one to "just put your name next to whatever you'd like," assuring us that she was happy knowing that it would continue to bring pleasure or render service.

She continued to go to church, meet with her bridge-club luncheon group, and talk with many people on the phone who were just hearing the news. Like us, they were struggling to comprehend the suddenness of this development and needed to talk, to hear more or speak with her.

Brothers and sisters and their spouses, nieces and nephews and cousins all came, some contributing a day, others a week, to keep my mother company. And at the end of each day, the one with her sent out an e-mail to all the others, relating the story of the day. One of my brothers captured the specialness of it:

Each day here has been so rich even in its quiet simplicity, and I am amazed by how even in their dying, Mother and Dad have called us to be family to and for one another—not in anything they say or request, but, literally, in how they die; they give us an opportunity to draw together around them and around each other. For me, their "ends" have provided "new beginnings" for the intra-family relationships that I have with all of you. Sometimes the deaths of parents rip families apart and create dissension among them over material goods and what not. Conversely, I am so struck by and so

grateful for the deeper love that I have come to have for each
of you through the experiences of our parents' dying.

Another brother, who enjoys treks on the St. Croix River in his
pontoon boat, offered in one of his nightly reports the image of
a "no-wake zone":

> that part of a lake or waterway where boats must slow down
> to idle speed so that no wake is created. In the no-wake zone,
> people and things move slowly, cautiously, carefully. The
> zone is calm and quiet because there is no revving of
> motors—motors are at idle speed, generating only enough
> rpm's to propel the vessel forward at a quiet and slow pace
> so as not to make waves and upset others' quiet enjoyment
> of the zone. It is a respectful area. Well, that fairly describes
> Mom's apartment in these days—it's a "no-wake zone."
> People and things move slowly and cautiously. It is a zone of
> relative quiet and calm. It is a place where all who enter are
> respectful...of life, of the dying process, of a life well lived. It
> is a safe haven.

Each of us eagerly went to our computers to get the daily
update on Mom's health, but along with that, we got to learn
about the family members who provided it with their genera-
tional perspectives. In seeing a situation through their eyes, hearing what they'd said or done, we got insights into them. One of
my brothers wrote, "I find myself awaiting each update more
than any gift I have received in years." We were like most families, caught up in our busy lives and having the opportunity to
share with one another only at special times like Christmas or
birthdays. But here, day after day for several weeks, there was a
value-laden, in-depth sharing of hearts and minds. We had never
been in closer communication and deeper solidarity with one
another. Throughout their marriage, Dad and Mom's first prior-
ity was family. And now, even in their dying, they were doing
what they had dedicated themselves to throughout their lives:
drawing us closer together in love.

When my turn to spend a week with Mom came around
again in mid-March, it was the middle of Lent, and I called and
asked her if she would be interested in making our week together

a kind of Lenten retreat. "I think that would be wonderful," she said. "I'm ready to step back and take a rest from all the activity of cleaning out closets and drawers and shelves." So I brought some resources home with me—films, music, readings—to sprinkle into each day as her energy and interest invited.

One afternoon I asked her if she would be interested in my leading her through a meditation on dying.

"What good does that do?" she asked.

"For some people, it helps tame their fears of death."

"I don't have any fear of death. I'm looking forward to it."

"You're actually *looking forward* to it?"

"Yes. I've had a good life." She proceeded to list all the blessings, and then said calmly, "I'm ready to let go when the time comes."

On St. Patrick's Day, some longtime family friends invited us over to their home for an Irish meal of corned beef and cabbage with boiled potatoes and key lime pie for dessert. On other days, friends would occasionally come by with a large cooler and proceed to unload a full-course meal in an amazing demonstration of love and generosity.

But the gift went both ways. One friend, Suzanne, sixty-six, who considered Mom a mentor, shared that watching how Mom was living her last months was freeing her from what she described as her lifelong fear of death. "I've been paranoid about it," she said, "and that's slowly dissolving as I visit your Mom."

Dr. Kübler-Ross, pioneer in the field of palliative and hospice care, wrote about the "symbolic language" of the dying, and provided numerous examples. In being home this time, I noticed that one of the things Mom was doing differently from the month previous was that when she was ready for bed, she would walk out into the hallway or living room and say, "OK, I'm ready to be tucked in now." So I would go in and tuck her in, and then place my hand on her head and offer a prayer of thanks for what we'd lived that day, and ask that she would have a peaceful night and good rest. Then, a good-night hug and kiss, and it was lights off. My "read" of this was that the "get it done/get my affairs in order" phase was ending, and she was ready just to *be* now, with loving touch, silent communion, heartfelt sharing, and a hug and kiss.

One of her granddaughters observed how inspiring it was to see—especially now—the "attitude of gratitude" out of which Mom lived: "She is so thankful for everything. Thankful for having us all be available to stay with her, thankful for eighty-eight healthy years, thankful for Jesus' closeness to her."

My gift to Mother at Christmas had been a plane ticket to come live Holy Week with me in Washington as she had done the previous year. The diagnosis that took us all by surprise five weeks later made that unrealistic. So at the end of March I came back a third time to spend Holy Week with her in Minnesota instead.

One of my brothers joined me for a meeting with the hospice nurse who was coming for her twice-weekly visit. Mom put on her black slacks and a lovely blouse. Her hair was primped, and her lips were touched up with red lipstick. The nurse was impressed with how well she was doing, but at the same time, she thought it would be good to have a walker, wheelchair, and oxygen machine and tanks delivered to the apartment "just so they're here when you need them." That very afternoon, a gentleman carried them into the living room and instructed me in their use while Mom sat on the sofa looking at this sudden incursion of equipment. It was a visual notice that we were on the cusp of a new phase, and Mom was taken aback by the prospect of it. In the evening we watched a family reunion video on the occasion of her and Dad's fiftieth anniversary, and she went to bed smiling.

The nurse must have been inspired with that equipment order, because the next morning Mom's legs were too weak to support her weight, and she used the walker to traverse the distance from her bedroom to the kitchen. By the afternoon, she needed the wheelchair, and after enjoying the soft breeze and birdsong of a beautiful sunny day, she asked to lie down again. By this time, several other family members had arrived, and we all gathered around her bed for another anointing and a time of prayer. Her mind was sharp, and she asked one granddaughter about her two boys and another about the home she and her husband had just purchased.

When darkness fell and all the family members had departed, I lay beside her on the bed. Between midnight and one o'clock in the morning, her breathing became more labored, and I wheeled in the oxygen machine and tanks, turned them on, and applied the breathing tubes to her nose. It seemed to help. Her breathing was becoming quieter—or was it just the noise from the oxygen machine that made it difficult for me to hear it? Then I noticed her chest was no longer rising and falling, and applied my fingers to her neck pulse...then put my ear to her heart. Nothing. It slowly began to break over me: She was not breathing. She had died.

Her diagnosis had been delivered shortly before Lent began, and it was now Holy Thursday, the day on which Christ instituted the Eucharist, the sacred meal that gave her strength and hope throughout her life. It is on the eve of this day that the Church begins its celebration of the Easter Triduum, the Three Great Days in which we celebrate Jesus' passing over through death to new, resurrected life and his opening the gates of eternal life in heaven for us all.

There *is* a Providence that guides our lives.

The way our parents died was their final gift and blessing to our family, faith community, and society. We're meant to give not only our lives for others, but our deaths as well. Just as parents and grandparents and teachers must coach the young in how to live, they are also called to teach them how to die. When we give that lesson to others, we die in such a way that our deaths are our final blessing to them.

How we perceive death affects the way we live. How we live affects the way we die. How we die gives new meaning to the way others can live.

Resources for Your Inner Work

Reflections

What have you received?

Every part of life teaches us, and death is a part of life. The loss of a parent teaches us just how valuable, precious, and special a human being can be. Your mother or father is, or was, different from everyone else in the world. There never was anyone just like him or her, and there never will be. The loss of a parent is so painful because of that uniqueness. But nobody ever dies completely. When someone dies, we discover how much he or she left behind—from clothing and furniture to recipes, stories, songs, prayers, and ways of doing things. The loved one will be part of us for the rest of our lives.

Make a list: If one or both of your parents have died, write down some of things that they left behind.

What do you believe?

Do you agree or disagree with each of the following statements?

1. Sharing the stages of the dying process with another can bring us increasingly closer to a level of acceptance of our own mortality.
2. Facing death means facing the ultimate questions of life's value and meaning. In the big picture of things, each of our lives is short, and everything we do counts.
3. Our encounters with the reality of death can enrich our lives more than any other experience we have had.
4. When the death of someone makes us very sad, we learn something new and important about how wonderful it is to be alive. Such an experience teaches us that life is sacred.
5. If we have the courage to deal with dying when it comes into our lives, to accept it as an important and valuable part of life, then we will grow—either through our own or another's dying.
6. The qualities that enable us to deal comfortably with death (compassion, love, courage, patience, hope, and faith) are the same ones that distinguish a growing human being at any stage of life.

What do you remember?

What stories do you have about the dying and the deaths of loved ones? What do they mean for your own attitude toward both life and death?

Exercises

Acknowledge the presence of death

The next time you go into town or to the store or out into your neighborhood for a walk, reflect on the fact that everyone you see will die—and that everyone you see is your brother or sister both in life and in death.

At the end of the day, reflect on whether opening your heart to this fact gave you a new attitude toward those you encountered.

Prepare your obituary

Using some obituaries from your local newspaper as models, write your own. Then provide a copy of it to those who would likely be responsible upon your death to provide an obituary about you to the newspapers.

What feelings do you have when you realistically consider your own death?

Plan your funeral

Consider this letter to the editor in *The New York Times* regarding an article titled "No Longer Avoiding That Talk about the Inevitable":

> One of the best gifts my mother gave my brother, two sisters and me was to plan her own funeral to the last detail. Her reasoning was that her wishes would be carried out this way. When she died at 85, her plans were in place. We were freed from the doubts of "What would mother want?" and could focus on comforting one another and her closest friends. Death is inevitable, but I am at peace knowing that my mother's wishes were honored with dignity and love.
>
> —C.L., Forest, Ill.[18]

In the Appendix at the back of this book, you will find a detailed guide to planning your own funeral.

Film

Watch *Two Weeks*, a 2007 motion picture starring Sally Fields, about a mother's dying and her three adult children who care for her.

Words to Live By

Death is not an enemy to be conquered or a prison to be escaped. It is an integral part of our lives that gives meaning to human existence. It sets a limit on our time in this life, urging us to do something productive with that time as long as it is ours to use. When you fully understand that each day you awaken could be the last you have, you take time that day to grow, to become more of who you really are, to reach out to other human beings.[19]   —*Elisabeth Kübler-Ross*

Poem

Death is not putting out the light.
It is only extinguishing a lamp
Because the day has come.

—*Rabindranath Tagore, Bengali philosopher, poet,
and winner of the Nobel Prize for literature in 1913*

The Glacier

Once from a boat's bow
I saw a giant crystal,
wide as the city limits
and high as a ski hill,
its turquoise pallor
striated with dark veins,
a vast field of fairy-chimneys
in fantastic formations of ice
—here an upward thrust
of praying hands, there
a Matterhorn-shaped minaret—
the whole of it a picture
of permanence.

Then suddenly sonic cracks
catalyze crystalline towers
tumbling them headlong into the sea,
bespeckling the agitated bay
with pulverized pinnacles and
quickly revealing the vulnerability
of all things fixed and frozen.
Wherever you sail from here,
remember this: however wide
and deep your grief,
it will recede.

Chapter Five

Grief, Ritual, and Growth

Loss and grief are inevitable. Growth is optional.
—R. Scott Sullender

The anticipated death of our elders certainly affects and touches us, but it generally does not surprise us. Their death might plunge us into sadness, but it may equally evoke our recognition of the beauty and richness of their lives. It's not that we would characterize every life as "beautiful," but in every life's unfolding, the struggles, errors, joys, and accomplishments give it a certain weight and, in the end, inspire respect.

But it also happens that people who are close to us die young, "too early," we say. There are deaths for which we can gradually prepare ourselves and accept, like at the end of a long sickness, for example. And there are others due to accidents, like a car collision or a plane crash, that knock the wind out of us by their suddenness or violence. Or it may be a suicide, revealing the deep suffering, either physical or psychological, of someone whom we may have done our best to accompany during a time of depression.

As we have seen in the chapter on practicing our little letting go's, all throughout life we suffer losses: material losses, as well as relational, functional, and role losses. Then, when someone close to us dies, we are faced with a Big Letting Go, and find ourselves enmeshed in a bewildering cluster of human emotions, intensified and complicated by virtue of our relationship to the one lost.

112

There is a difference between sorrow and grief. Sorrow is occasioned by the ordinary disappointments, losses, regrets of living. Grief, on the other hand, is deep sorrow caused by unusual loss. Grief is more acute than sorrow and is oftentimes marked by passionate demonstrations of feelings. Grieving is to *be* in sorrow. To lament. To feel distress. To mourn. Grieving is a process of sorrowing deeply over a period of time. There are long-term aftershocks, and they come in spasms. A memory, a smell, a song, a "look alike," an anniversary can trigger a surge of emotions. As the poet Edna St. Vincent Millay wrote, "The presence of that absence is everywhere."[1]

Grieving—the painful physical, emotional, and spiritual journey that we go through to come to terms with the loss of someone through death, separation, or divorce—is among the most sacred and most human things we will ever undergo. It plunges us into the mysteries of life. The person who is dead has been freed from illness and pain and suffering, but we who live on have not. Jesus knew something of the glory he was called to, but we simply do not. We do not know where our loved ones have been taken to, and we want them back. The pain of separation is intense, as it was for Jesus' friends after they lost him. Pain is inseparable from love: that is a truth we must live with.

There is no set pattern of "normal" grief responses. Some people eat a lot; others very little. Some sleep a lot; others do not. Some withdraw into isolation; others are in constant need of people around them. Some people look mad. Some look sad. Some look distant. Whatever form it takes is "normal" for that person. Grief is a roller coaster; there's nothing sane or predictable about it. The average time frame for grieving is several months in the case of an expected death and a year when death was unexpected; but in actuality, grieving can take years. And there's no pushing the river. It will take the time it takes.

Some behavior may not look like grief and can be confusing, even frustrating, for friends and family, but grieving underlies it. People who are grieving may look okay, but when you get underneath the surface with them, you find out they're not sleeping or they're angry at coworkers or they're fighting with family. Some get very active and help those around them, while others withdraw into seclusion. Some want to talk about it a great deal. At the same time, there are styles of grief—like getting overly busy or rationalizing away the sense of loss and the need to grieve—that, while numbing the pain, do not favor the healing within.

Grief is a loss of connection, a connection that gave meaning to our lives. Now I have to decide: What am I living for? What gives me a reason to get up in the morning? Where's the meaning in my life? Experts say the best way to help those who are grieving is to spend time *being with* and *listening* to them rather than *talking to* them. Grief is best healed in community. Supported by a community, the grieving person will find it easier to let go of what is over, to harvest the experience for its wisdom, to tell the story until he or she does not have to tell it anymore. Grieving is more a matter of the heart than of the head.

Open Your Eyes

Dick Eggers wrote about the death of his adult son, Tom. The story reveals how sometimes, as people talk, they hear themselves say things that clarify their reactions or feelings. In Dick's case, he was grieving the imminent loss of a son who was still alive.

Tom was thirty-three, married just a year and a half, active and seemingly healthy, but then began experiencing some stomach pains. Tom went to the doctor who ordered an immediate CAT scan, which revealed stage four stomach cancer that had spread to his liver and lungs. Three months later, Dick was on the floor of a New York City hospital where the terminal patients stayed, massaging his dying son's feet, and he found himself screaming at God in his mind:

> Where was God? How could he be letting this happen? And wasn't I worthy of this healing for my son, after all these years of serving God and his people and standing up for our faith?
>
> "…Where is this healing love of yours? Show yourself! You owe it to *me*, God!"

In between my rants, I slowly became aware of something—a small quiet voice, barely understood, almost a whisper: "Open your eyes!"

My vision was blurred by tears, but as I took in the familiar scene in that hospital room, I finally understood what I was witnessing. It was the very presence of our loving God in the form of the people who were standing and kneeling all around Tom.

What I had so wanted to see—God's healing love making Tom whole—had been happening before my eyes, though not in the way I had expected. Tom's wife, his mother, his brother and sisters, his friends, and even me—we ourselves were the reality of God's love.

The doctors and nurses had told us very clearly that Tom would not have lasted so long without our loving him as we did. And now I could see the spiritual dimension of this love. All of us together were the hands and heart of God, weeping, holding Tom's hands, stroking his head, kissing him, telling him how much we loved him.

God was so very present in that room! It virtually glowed with the Holy Spirit.[2]

Eggers went on to recount how the wake—attended by 2,400 people—and the funeral were a blur, but etched in his memory was every detail of that epiphany moment when, in Tom's hospital room, he saw God truly present and at work through his people. Dick saw that "in his dying, Tom was being truly healed and made whole; he was being born into eternal life." Dick's story also reveals how one's belief system can be significantly altered or challenged by loss, and then not only restored but strengthened. In his words:

This healing did not stop with Tom. God's love is very much at work within our family, affecting our relationships with one another and with Tom's friends. It has brought my wife and I so very much closer. It has allowed us to be present to comfort others who have experienced similar losses. All of us are slowly beginning to understand that God is the giver of life, not death, and that his wisdom far exceeds our ability to comprehend dying.[3]

In the grieving process, attachments to the lost person or object are not entirely given up, but are sufficiently altered to permit the grieving person to admit the reality of the loss and to live without constant reference to it. The deep feelings aroused by the loss are acknowledged and relatively fully expressed. The mourner gradually becomes able to invest in other persons and things again. And, as witnessed to in Dick's story, a belief system, significantly altered or challenged by loss, is restored.

The tasks of mourning associated with this process are to accept the reality of the loss, to experience the pain of grief, to adjust to the environment where the deceased is missing, and to take the energy of grieving and reinvest it in someone or something worthwhile. When these tasks are effectively engaged, the "victories" that come are restoration of energy for living, restoration to significant community, and restoration of meaning.

Grief and Growth

In his book *Grief and Growth*,[4] R. Scott Sullender develops the relationship between the two. We tend to see grief and growth as opposite ends of the spectrum when, in fact, loss, bereavement, and suffering can be the trigger for tremendous growth and creativity. Our structured lives are thrown into chaos, and so we work to create restructuring, sense, and meaning in our lives.

Growth means "change." As we recover from grief, we do not return to being the same person that we were before. As Dick's story witnesses, we have grown and changed. The key is to change in a health-oriented direction. Growth should be in a direction that increases our perception of reality, including our awareness, our self-acceptance, and our capacity for love. To repeat Scott's words, which opened this chapter, "Loss and grief are inevitable. Growth is optional."

Growth is like a voyage. It involves leaving home, traveling to new places inside ourselves, and returning home with an expanded awareness. Just as leaving home involves letting go of our commitments and involvements, of our secure identity or cherished beliefs, so can the grieving process involve this. We begin to see the world in a new way.

Being in a strange country means that the old patterns and maps don't make sense. When in a new setting, we can experience panic, confusion, and pain. We instinctively seek that which is familiar and secure. It takes courage to grow when we can't see the other side of the mountain. Growth involves risk, which means that we must be people of courage and faith. And in the end, we do return to the place we have left, but with a new, expanded sense of the world and our place in it. The growth cycle is never complete until we integrate the new knowledge and experiences into our old identity.

In order to grow through our losses, we need a sense of freedom, responsibility, and choices. We can choose, for example, to grieve or not to grieve, how we will grieve, with whom and when.

If we are accompanying others who are grieving, we may be able to recognize unhealthy behaviors. It might look like poor personal care and hygiene, or fatigue, depression, and lack of social interaction or interest. Since we're there to support the person, not to judge him or her, the best approach may be to simply try to get the person to clarify the behavior. Asking why he or she is acting a certain way may not help; it is difficult for people who are grieving to step back and give a reflective account of their behavior because everything is affected by the whirlpool of their emotions. But if we simply describe to the person the behavior that we are seeing and name the possible underlying emotions, it may help his or her own understanding of what is happening or driving the behavior. We can't force someone to do anything, but we can help the person recognize what he or she is doing. Growth comes when we recognize our choices, assume responsibility for our lives, and don't let fate control us.

Our attitude makes the difference. God has given us the capacity to be responsible for our lives and those we love by means of the choices that we make. Grief is past oriented, yet it sets the stage for growth, which is future oriented. We cannot go forward until we have let go of the past and recovered our emotional energy to reinvest in the future.

Grief is a long-term process. There may be a sense of it being finished, yet it is never finished. One seeks to incorporate into one's life what has happened and then go on to reinvest, restore, recycle one's energies, and risk loving again. It's not uncommon for women and men to grieve differently. Women generally cry more easily and need to talk to other women. Men tend to find it more difficult to express their pain and cry less frequently. They are more likely to express their grief through an action like planting a tree or erecting a monument.

Life will always be filled with problems, difficulties, losses, "little deaths." We have a choice: to see them as stumbling blocks or stepping stones. Our choice can make all the difference. There's truth to the adage that "time heals pain," but time doesn't do it by itself. We have to work at the process, make constructive, life-enhancing choices even when we don't feel like it. We cannot change the circumstances of loss, but we do have something to say about how we will respond to the circumstances in which we now find ourselves.

Grief is a process and it is hard work, but it is worth the effort because we and our lives are worth the effort. How we recover from grief depends upon our inner resources and on the support we receive from others. Grief is the price we pay for love, and it can be the source of much growth and gain. Some widows and widowers, once greatly dependent on their spouses, find themselves growing as they are forced to discover inner strength, acquire new skills, and play unfamiliar roles. The person who is lost can never be replaced, but that doesn't mean we can never love again.

The Church:
A Community of Memory

In modern Western society, the two institutions that have had the most influence on how people face death are hospitals and funeral homes. And in the process of their expanding role, the communal practices that once surrounded this life passage have also undergone some changes. For example, most cultures lived much closer to the fact of human mortality, and people died in their homes, surrounded by family. But now that we live longer, we increasingly tend to die in hospitals and palliative-care centers. The capabilities of modern medicine to extend life present us with new scenarios that sometimes aid, and sometimes render more difficult, our chances of dying well. On the one hand, medical teams are ready to try high-risk physical cures; on the other, the hospice movement represents an effort to shift the focus away from the disease and back to the person. There are, however, other kinds of hope to offer dying persons.

This was once the domain of church communities. It still is, though less so today. Hospitals have largely supplanted families in the care of the sick, while the formal acknowledgment of death and a response to grief have been given over to funeral homes. Funeral homes have developed a large range of services from custodial care of the body to wakes, funeral, and memorial and burial services. In doing so, they fill a void in modern Western society: people want and need communal practices that honor the dead and bring consolation to the grieving.

But, for those who belong to it, the Church is a community of memory in a way that the hospital and the funeral home are not. In the Church community, the names and faces of the departed are carried in prayer at the time of, and long after, their passing. Through prayers, visits, and meals for the family, the Christian community offers a depth of spiritual and practical support that neither funeral home nor hospital can match.

Lament and Hope, Judgment and Mercy

Christians have ministered to the dying and the bereaved for two thousand years. The Christian tradition's view of death is complex. When our practices are healthy, they are marked by four characteristics: lament and hope, on the one hand, and on the other, a sense of divine judgment and an awareness of divine mercy.[5]

Lament

Not everyone dies peacefully and of old age. Lives are often cut short by war, disease, accidents, suicide. We lament because we value so highly God's gift of earthly life. We lament because death does separate us from those we love on earth; it is a wrenching loss for those who are left behind. But it is also a loss to those who know they are dying—loss of the possibilities they envisioned for the future, of the relationships they delighted in. Lament, however, is balanced by hope and thanksgiving.

The approach of death can be a time of thanksgiving for all God's gifts during our lives. In *Tuesdays with Morrie*, the terminally ill patient Morrie invites all his friends over to the house for a party *before* he dies. He doesn't want to be dead when they celebrate his life and gifts to them; he wants to hear what they say and express gratitude for their gifts to him, too. Wakes and funerals are also a time to remember the accomplishments and good efforts of the dead, a time to celebrate their gifts and legacy.

Hope

We can also speak about death in terms of gain as well as loss. We believe that true human fulfillment occurs only on the other side of this life. The fundamental Christian conviction is that death marks the point at which temporal obstacles to our experience of God's love pass away. Sharing the ritual meal of the Eucharist at this time is particularly appropriate because in this sacrament, both Christ's willing brokenness for our sake and God's promise of new life are made vividly present.

But there is another sense to our hope, too. Although death is part of our natural condition, it is not something with which we are fully at peace. We find comfort in knowing that God is actively working against the powers of death in all creation. The promise that gives us hope is that in God's kingdom there will be no more suffering, no more sorrow, no more tears, no more death.

> For the trumpet will sound, and the dead will be raised imperishable, and we will be changed....When this perishable body puts on imperishability, and this mortal body puts on immortality, then the saying that is written will be fulfilled:
>   "Death has been swallowed up in victory."
>   "Where, O death, is your victory?
>   Where, O death, is your sting?" (1 Cor 15:52, 54–55)

Will the final and definitive transformation happen at the end of time or immediately after death? If, according to the traditional faith, our bodies will rise at the end of the world, we must at the same time acknowledge that we have no idea what this "end" corresponds to in the new and already-present world in which the risen Christ lives. And since we know that we are already united here below in the Holy Spirit with the body of the risen Christ, we are able to believe that directly after death we shall find in this uninterrupted union the source and means of our essential blessedness.[6]

Our hope derives from knowing that death, for all its power to separate and alienate, will be part of the old order that passes away. In the meantime, we are to resist the powers of death at work in the world through injustice, exploitation, and violence.

Judgment

While we do understand death as a natural part of our finitude as creatures, we also learn from scripture that death is due to our sinfulness (as in the Adam and Eve story). The writings of Paul state clearly that "death spread to all because all have sinned" (Rom 5:12). However sin originated and spread, it is clear that, unchecked, it distorts and destroys our relationships and us. This means that we need to acknowledge God's judgment and seek God's forgiveness. Confessing our sins and asking for forgiveness should be regular occurrences in the Christian life, but when death approaches, these practices assume a heightened sense of urgency and significance.

People often feel a deep and instinctive need for forgiveness at the end of their lives. The imminence of death is often the occasion for reconciliation with others that we may have been avoiding for years. Some dying people hang on, waiting for the opportunity to heal a breach with a family member or to say the words to a son or daughter that were always so hard to say. Kathleen Fischer describes forgiveness as a layered process:

> The process of forgiveness is hard to describe because it takes as many twists and turns as an individual life. Understanding the meaning of an injury in our lives takes time and includes many levels of insight into our pain and the meaning of letting go. It is a layered process, and does not have to be total to be helpful. Forgiveness does not mean that we overlook offenses and pretend they never happened; nor that we give up protection of self. We need only begin the process, be open to healing, and pray for the grace of forgiveness; the rest will come.
>
> One therapist suggests four stages of forgiveness: to forgo (leave it alone), to forbear (to abstain from punishing), to forget (to avert from memory, to refuse to dwell), to forgive (to abandon the debt).... Our part in the process is to refuse to dwell, to punish, to recollect. We stop bringing up the wrong again and again, and make a conscious decision not to hold resentment and retaliate.
>
> Forgiveness of another paradoxically frees us from their power to determine our lives. As long as our energy is absorbed in hatred and resentment, it is unavailable to us for other things. Forgiveness restores us to our selves; we can center on our own desires and live out of them.[7]

Taking the memory of a hurt or the specific need for forgiveness into the sacrament of reconciliation is a means of opening the wounded part of one's spirit to the healing power of Christ.

Mercy

Divine judgment and divine mercy do not have equal weight in Christian reflections on death. We worship a God who "does not deal with us according to our sins" (Ps 103:10). The chief way of providing a dying person with a profound experience of God's mercy is through a caring presence, a skilled and compassionate ministry to their bodily and spiritual needs. Anointing the sick with oil embodies God's mercy toward the dying in words and actions, and words of pardon and peace acknowledge the human need for forgiveness.

One of the ways in which the mercy of Christ can be incarnated is by loving care for the body. The interconnections between body and spirit are deep. Those who work with terminally ill patients can rightfully see their work as "an opportunity to express God's mercy to the dying by faithful and loving care of the body, which becomes increasingly more difficult to care for and often repulsive. But if [we] remain loving and faithful to that task until the end, the dying person has received a life-giving experience" of God's compassion and mercy.[8]

This caring presence also invites loving support of the person's spirit. Playing soothing music, hanging a comforting picture in the line of vision, saying prayers or singing hymns that lift the heart, taking the person to a window to look out on nature's beauty are all examples of concrete ways of tenderly massaging another's spirit.

The Role of Ritual

Various sociocultural shifts are currently affecting the way we view sickness and death. As technology advances, there is a tendency to see illness and dying as medical science's sphere of activity. Seniors often live removed from their relatives and their accustomed environment, and their funeral services may be prearranged and not include a service in church. Large funeral establishments offer a complete line of services to the family of the deceased, including a chapel available for religious services. And when people's own level of religious observance has fallen off, they tend to forgo church celebrations of customary funeral rites.

Todd Van Beck, an educator, writer, and speaker in the funeral profession, contends that people who do not go through the funeral process give job security to psychiatrists. The money not spent on a funeral will be spent in counseling down the road. He believes we are facing a crisis of ritual in our society. Increasingly, people are unchurched and no longer see the meaning in the ritual. They live fast-paced lives with shallow attachments in a disposable society, and want to treat death in a like manner. They will instinctively want to care for the dead in the way they live their lives: quickly and efficiently. But death and the grieving process are different. They require slowing down. Ceremonies and rituals are important to mark key events, both of joy and of sorrow.[9]

Ritual is a structured activity that facilitates personal and social transactions. Varieties of ritual behaviors enable humans to feel at home with themselves, with others, and with life's environment in general. Humans learn ritual behaviors as part of the process of socialization. From time immemorial, people have given the highpoints of their existence a festal or significant form. When someone is born or reaches majority age or gets married or dies, the event is signaled by a celebration that contrasts with the grayness of everyday life. There is a spontaneous effort to create forms that will celebrate the significance of life and of particular moments in our lives. During rituals, we think of what we are and celebrate our existence.

The Christian Funeral Rites

Religious rituals (generally called rites), like social rituals, are intended to be formative and expressive of personal and communal identity. This identity is one that requires initiation into the meanings of the rituals, for the form or the structure of a ritual conveys meaning greater than the sensible form itself. In baptism, for example, the primary sensible form is the pouring of water over the one baptized. But this ritual action carries a meaning greater than simply cleansing; it encompasses belonging and sharing in the very life of God. In other words, religious rituals are symbolic actions that unify the performer of those actions with the sacred.

The funeral rites permit the community of the living to confer a place to the deceased in, for example, confiding him to God or burying her in the earth. The rites also help the community reorganize itself so as to continue to live in the person's absence. The bereaved need the time accorded by the rites to absorb and integrate the fact that life will no longer be as "before." They also need a supportive space in which they will be recognized in both their grief and their new identity.

And the community, for its part, needs the time and space to honor the life of the one who has departed. The rites place us each in our own way before our fragility, and evoke emotions that need expression while also offering us meaning and hope.

In Christian history, the funeral rites have reflected a variety of theological and spiritual sensibilities. In the Catholic tradition there is the sprinkling with water in remembrance of the deceased person's initiation into the community of faith, an incensing of the body, and the placing of a white cloth on the coffin signifying life in Christ. Among the gestures proper to Orthodox tradition is the incensing and anointing of the body with oil and earth, as well as a kiss given to the deceased as an expression of love for the departed and an affirmation that the one who has died, having lived a life of faith and having known the grace of God, is worthy of the fulfillment of God's promises. In the Protestant tradition, the accent placed on the hope of the resurrection leads to less importance being accorded to the body in the funeral service, which in certain traditions may correspondingly be called a service of thanksgiving.

Christians celebrate the funeral rites to offer worship, praise, and thanksgiving to God for the gift of the life that has just been returned to God, the author of life. In the Catholic tradition, the funeral usually takes place within the context of the Eucharist, the memorial of the death and resurrection of Christ. It consoles the bereaved with the encouraging words of the biblical readings and with the sacrament of holy communion.

While proclaiming the gospel of Jesus Christ and witnessing to Christian hope in the resurrection, the
funeral rites affirm and express the union of the
Church on earth with the Church in heaven in the one
great communion of saints. Though separated from
us, those who have passed through death's door are
still one with the community of believers on earth and
benefit from their prayers and intercessions. The community recognizes the spiritual bond that still exists
and proclaims its belief that all the faithful will be
raised up and reunited in the reign of God where
death will be no more.[10]

Coming to the church for these rites makes all the sense in
the world for the believer who has celebrated the significant
moments of his or her life there: baptism, confirmation, marriage. It is there that faith in the resurrection has been nourished
through scripture and Eucharist, there that sins have been con-
fessed and pardon received. The whole journey of faith finds its
natural culmination in the final rites of passage.

The Christian burial rites are appropriately comprehensive
in their scope. They encompass the comforting of the mourners,
prayers at the funeral home, the closing of the coffin, entrance to
church, worship, the sprinkling and incensing the body of the
deceased, and the last farewell at the cemetery.

In and through these rites in which the Christian community commends the deceased to God, the faith of the participants is actively engaged and strengthened as they reflect on the
deep mystery of our lives: every new experience of life only
comes to us through an experience of dying. The Church calls
this the paschal mystery, the mystery of *pascha* or "passing over"
from death to life.

Ministry of Consolation

When a member of the Church dies, the faithful are called to a
ministry of consolation to those who have suffered the loss of a
loved one. The believing community acts on the words and

example of Jesus: "Blessed are those who mourn, for they will be comforted" (Matt 5:4). The community's principal involvement in the ministry of consolation is expressed in its active participation in the celebration of the funeral rites, particularly the vigil of the deceased, the funeral liturgy, and the rite of committal.

The family can and should be involved in planning the funeral rites: in the choice of texts and rites for the ritual, in the selection of music, and in the designation of liturgical ministers. These rites should normally be scheduled at times that permit as many of the community as possible to be present. The assembly's participation can be assisted by preparation of booklets that contain an outline of the rite, the texts, and songs belonging to the people, as well as instructions for posture, gesture, and movement.[11]

The *Order of Christian Funerals* offers these perspectives:

In every celebration of the dead, the Church attaches great importance to the reading of the word of God. The readings proclaim to the assembly the paschal mystery, teach remembrance of the dead, convey hope of being gathered together again in God's kingdom, and encourage the witness of Christian life....A careful selection and use of readings from scripture will provide the family and the community with an opportunity to hear God speak to them in their needs, sorrows, fears, and hopes. (22)

Having heard the word of God proclaimed and preached, the assembly responds...with prayers for the deceased and all the dead, for the family and all who mourn, and for all in the assembly....Confident in their belief in the communion of saints, [they] exercise their royal priesthood by joining together in this prayer for all those who have died. (29)

Music is integral to the funeral rites. It allows the community to express convictions and feelings that words alone may fail to convey. It has the power to console and uplift the mourners and to strengthen the unity of the assembly in faith and love. The texts of the songs chosen for a particular celebration should express the paschal mystery of the Lord's suffering, death, and triumph over death and should be related to all the readings from scripture. (30)

Ritual and Healthy Grieving

Funerals are always for the living. The living gather together to remember, to share the story of the loved one, and to be supported by the living God. We stand needy, searching for direction and support in all our emotional upheaval and tears. The process of the funeral is meant to help us come to terms with the pain of the loss and find hope even in our sorrow.

Grief can never be hurried or fixed into neat time slots. Only when we have worked through this suffering can our regular life be regained once again. The pain of the loss will fade but not disappear. We learn to live in a new way without the loved one's physical presence. We live and work into the meaning that the rituals of dying bring.

The funeral rituals are best not confined to the liturgy in the church. We also need to develop rituals that are user-friendly for the home. It might be a daily prayer service for the family, around the table together, each day leading up to the funeral and during the month following it.

The rituals are the tools of communication that we use to convey and move into the deeper meaning of life. Our rituals give us a means of expression when we have no words. Not surprisingly, it is through ritual that we communicate with the Divine, who is beyond all words. It is in ritual that we can open ourselves to the workings of God in our lives. They are carriers of grace and strength in this time of confusion. Their power comes from their ability to evoke from deep within the individual the experience of God's presence.

The funeral rituals are not merely actions we do, but rather the way that we live through the pain and suffering of death and separation.

Seven Ritual Elements for Healthy Grieving[12]

1. Encountering

The funeral is a liturgy of worship. It should not be rushed. We come to be touched and shaped by God. The centrally placed cross, Easter candle, and lectionary remind us that we have come to meet and interact with our God—powerful Creator, Redeemer, and life-giving Spirit.

The liturgy leaves no doubt that it is Christ who leads us. We have been baptized into the life and mystery of Jesus Christ. He has died and risen for us. Now we pray that the fullness of the mystery of Christ be made real for the deceased.

Our prayers make it clear that it is God whom we ask to forgive our sins and it is always his Son who will lead us to eternal life. We cannot do this by ourselves. This is all about what God is accomplishing in us through Christ. As we share in his very life here on earth, we also share in the promise of the resurrection.

2. Listening

The word of God is always central to our funeral liturgies. With a very human voice, God is speaking to us. The gathered congregation is attentive to God's word and is called to give concrete expression through their living and outreach to the bereaved of the ways God's Spirit is a Spirit of consolation, support, encouragement, forgiveness, and challenge.

3. Giving Thanks

When we come to the time of the funeral, all families are encouraged to remember the loved one, to tell the stories with gratefulness in their hearts. It is the spirit of gratitude that we bring as we make farewell. We speak our gratitude to God and to one another for the life of the deceased, however long or short it was. The love of this person was a gift in our lives. The funeral liturgy calls us to make this thanksgiving explicit and particular. We are people who are deeply loved and wanted by God. The prayers convey the feelings of gratitude that are in our hearts.

As we worship and give thanks to God, we express our appreciation for the blessing the deceased has been, and we beg forgiveness of our sins and the sins of the one who has died.

4. Remembering

The time leading up to and following the funeral liturgy is filled with storytelling. We have many great memories that we want to share with each other. In today's urban environment where efficiency is so highly valued, there can be undue emphasis on keeping the funeral "short and simple." We take off work for a couple hours and then hurry back to the office. We do violence to our own grieving process by cutting short the time we need to remember, to share, to laugh, and to cry over the deceased's life.

Our grandparents and great-grandparents came from a slower-moving world, but they were responding to a deep wisdom in coming together for several days when someone in the community died. In these gatherings there was opportunity to tell stories, eat, pray, and spend time with the loved one and the family. When it came time to take the body of the deceased to the church for the funeral, they had done all the storytelling they needed to do at that time. In the present configuration of events, the best opportunity for such is the wake service the afternoon and evening before the funeral.

5. Forgiving

No rite of passage should skirt around the tough issues of our relationship with the deceased. There may be situations when the gathered people need to reach out in forgiveness to the deceased, and the family and the gathered people toward each other. If there have been situations where the deceased was neglectful of and hurtful to some family members, the funeral can be a moment of healing and forgiveness if we but allow the pain and suffering to surface and bring it before God and one another. In the midst of all the pain, we bring the forgiving and healing power of God. This in turn can empower us to forgive one another.

The funeral can also be the occasion for healing in our relationship with each other. Against the backdrop of life and death, the grievances we carry are put in perspective, and we feel the desire to move forward unshackled in our relationships with others. The grace of God breaks through in unexpected and liberating ways. The Sign of Peace at Mass is always a strong moment to become conscious of the healing ways of God.

6. Surrendering

The journey to the cemetery helps everyone come to grips with reality. The loved one has died and will never return to be with us in the way we are accustomed. Painfully, with tears, we let go. We say good-bye.

The final prayers over the grave speak out our confidence in God: Bless these mortal remains and their resting place. Let perpetual light shine upon our loved one. What falls into the earth is only meant to be the seeds of eternal life. We are meant for a much greater glory.

This is the power that our faith brings to us: we can walk away from the cemetery with confidence. In all our tears, God will transform the pain of death into the birth pains of eternal life. We surrender our loved one into the hands of a loving God whom we trust to make real the promises made to us through Jesus Christ when we were baptized. "If we have died with Christ, we believe we will also live with him" (Rom 6:8). We return to the changed reality of our life now, but without being shackled by inconsolable grief.

7. Embracing

A healthy time of grieving, of encountering the living God, and of handing the loved one over to God must lead to embracing daily life once again. We can endure the pain, the emptiness, and the loss because we have walked through the suffering with our God and with many others who also share the pain and loss.

This experience of compassion and solidarity now becomes our strength, encouragement, and support to move again to living.

A healthy funeral does not deny the pain and suffering, nor the time that it will take to fully embrace life again. This is where the wisdom and practice of the Church has been so helpful. We live within the Communion of Saints. No one is ever meant to be forgotten. This need to remember is extended each Sunday where in our communal prayer we remember those who have gone before us.

The funeral ritual has power beyond our understanding. The readings, prayers, hymns, preaching, and ritual actions serve to make possible a healthy grieving. The deeper reality of giving the loved one over to God and letting go are aided by the prayer and worship of the gathered congregation that surrounds the family. Healthy grieving is always the servant of life well lived with God and one another.

Sharing Our Stories

Funerals are very significant moments in the life of every family, and each funeral is unique because of the deceased's history, role in the family, and influence on the larger community. But whatever shape a funeral may take, it is only when a family has grieved well that they will appreciate how life-giving the Christian rituals of death can be. The experience of living through these rites of passage will look and feel a little different to everyone who enters into them. The configuration and coloration of events will vary according to a variety of factors, such as the relationships among the family members, their relationship to the deceased and to the Church, and even the time of the year. Everyone who has lived the experience of loss and grief has a story of strength, consolation, comfort to share with others.

One of the gifts we can offer to one another is to share our stories about what it was like for us—the support given by friends and church community, the inspiration accruing from the memories recounted of the deceased, the consolation found in the service, the mysterious presence of grace surfacing in surprising ways. We are always learning, and sometimes we hear or see something that gives us an idea that may be helpful to us further down the line. Stories incarnate in more human terms the seven elements contained in healthy grieving cited above.

In that spirit, let me share with you what it was like for my own family to enter into the process of grieving and transition as we lived the days that immediately followed the death of our father and, not long after, the death of our mother, and how these elements of healthy grieving and the rituals of the wake, funeral, and burial supported us in that process.

On the morning after my father's death, November 2, we had a long, lovely liturgy on the feast of All Souls around the family table where Dad had always been a fixture. There was, of course, lots of singing. We simply put a Kleenex box in the middle of the table, and we were all invited to just let our emotions flow as they surfaced, and we did.

Mother's death occurred on Holy Thursday, and the liturgies of the Easter Triduum—Holy Thursday, Good Friday, Easter Sunday—provided rich reflections on death and resurrection, as well as a spacious structure for our grieving spread out over four days before her wake and funeral were held. The built-in quiet day of Holy Saturday was a particular gift. It was a very special time, all the more so by virtue of our sharing the language and experience of faith, which anchored our grieving in hope. The ritual provided a structured, safe opportunity for reflection upon what we were living and an opportunity for conscious integration.

The day following each one's death, we divvied up the tasks before us: prepare the service; make decisions about food for the reception and flowers for the funeral; work on the eulogy; organize travel arrangements for the grandchildren coming in; arrange the photo displays of family history; deliver the clothing chosen for burial to the mortuary. In the course of the day, people appeared at the door at the rate of about one an hour with baskets and bags of food. "What a lovely outpouring of the exchange of goods in the Communion of Saints!" my sister exclaimed.

In the evening, we sat close to one another, looking through family photo albums, letting the waves of emotion pass through, and letting each other feel the touch of caring hands.

The vigils before my parents' respective funerals included sharing memories—many wonderful stories from young and old that lifted up their social side and reflected on their faith and commitment to family and church community—and culminated in a prayer service including song, a reading, prayers of intercession, and a blessing.

At the end of my father's wake service, one of my fellow priests in our community in Washington, who had come to be with me, stood up and invited everyone to reflect on what had happened in the telling of the stories—how inspiration was given, how we needed to continue with this process and not let it stop with the end of the service, how we need to continue to share with one another the things that inspire us about the lives of others in the Communion of Saints and keep holding up those inspiring examples.

On the day of each funeral, once we were at our places in the church and the liturgy got underway, I experienced a strength that enabled me to lead the prayers and preach, keeping the focus on prayer for the deceased and off the emotion of this particular family member. The choir director told me afterward it was challenging emotionally for the choir, too, because both my parents had sung with them for so many years. It was wonderful seeing all the family members and friends come up in the communion line, coming to the table where all the saints gather. My sister delivered the eulogy for Dad, and shared that role with another brother at Mom's funeral.

After each burial, the whole extended family gathered in the evening for more sharing of stories and memories. Before going to bed I wrote in my journal, "What a tribute to the human spirit to run the gamut of emotions we traversed today—from the grief and tears of the closing of the casket, funeral and burial, to the laughter and levity of singing the favorite songs and eating the favorite food of one of our beloved parents!"

All in all, the events of those days were the most palpable experience of grace I've ever lived. And that was not something I ever expected. We all eventually went back to our home places and reengaged with our lives and work, but we continue to quietly ponder the mystery of grief and growth, the power of ritual, and God's presence and work in us through it all.

My Father's Funeral

I always wondered
whether I'd be at the altar
or in the pew with my family
among the mourners
at my father's funeral.

The hospital nurse understood:
You're more son
than priest here, she said;
And yet the two were melded into one.

In the pre-dawn on the morning of,
a dampened pillow muffled sobs
so as not to awaken a brother
sleeping in the next bed.

And only hours after,
sitting in a chair
rehearsing homiletic words,
the waves of emotion
continued to roll through
and break upon an inner beach.

It was only an hour before
the church began to fill
that I became aware of
a peaceful strength flowing in
from somewhere Beyond.

And when others respectfully probed
in the aftermath and said
That must have been hard
All I could do was say
The grace was given.

Resources for Your Inner Work

Funeral Arrangements

In the Appendix of this book, you will find a detailed resource for planning your own funeral as a gift to family members who would otherwise be faced with having to guess at what you would have liked.

Reflections

1. Who are the people whose deaths have most affected me?
2. Are there still "living traces" in my life of my relationship with them?
3. Write a page "In Memory of [name]." What are the salient events or moments shared that spring to mind? What were some of the person's memorable phrases or sayings, as well as noteworthy habits? What gave him or her joy? What is it about this person's life for which forgiveness and healing is still needed and/or for which I am grateful?
4. Who are the people in my life now that I deeply appreciate, but to whom I do not very frequently convey it?
5. Here are six "words" it is important for us to say to one another in order to die in peace or to allow another to die peacefully. Which of them do we use the most frequently in our interpersonal relations, and which do we neglect and want to learn to say more often?

   I forgive you.
   Please forgive me.
   Bravo! (a word of affirmation for something another has done)
   I love you.
   Thank you.
   Good-bye.

Prayer

God of all consolation,
In your unending love and mercy for us
you turn the darkness of death
into the dawn of new life.

Show your compassion to your people in their sorrow.
Be our refuge and our strength
to lift us from the darkness of this grief
to the peace and light of your presence.

Your son, our Lord Jesus Christ,
by dying for us, conquered death
and by rising again, restored life.

May we then go forward eagerly to meet him,
and after our life on earth
be reunited with our brothers and sisters
where every tear will be wiped away.[13]

Easter

The frigid compress of winter
came in layers of ice
around the turn of the year,
sheets of freezing rain
that fell for days
and chilled one's soul,
laying down a burden of crystal death,
forcing trees to bow low
in painful compliance
and finally crack
like brittle bones,
pinning bushes to the ground
with a vice-like grip
of cold-blooded strangulation.

Comes the longed-for warmth of Spring:
an April Easter Sunday
sitting in the garden
surrounded by fallen limbs
and entire uprooted trees,
surveying a hillside of brush
with spines forever crushed.

A cardinal fills the air
with birdsong
from a surviving branch above
and a robin dances amidst
an astonishment of crocus
pushing up prodigiously
through the chaotic cover
of twigs and leaves—

sheaves of green
piercing the thawing earth
and opening delicate petals
of blue rebirth
as once again
the message bursts forth
from the tomb of death:
Life reigns!

Chapter Six

Life After Death

*We do not live to ourselves, and we do not die to ourselves.
If we live, we live to the Lord, and if we die, we die to the
Lord; so then, whether we live or whether we die, we are
the Lord's. For to this end Christ died and lived again, so
that he might be Lord of both the dead and the living.*

—Romans 14:7–9

The end is not simply more of the middle. The end, in Christian perspective, really is an end. Death and eternity are not simply prolongations of what went before. The Gospels hint at this when they depict the risen Christ as both alike and unlike the Jesus the disciples knew before the crucifixion.

For the Christian faith, something definitive attaches to death. One is not simply exiting in order to start another phase of the karmic cycle. One is not simply leaving to join the world of universal archetypes. Persons are unrepeatable events. The death of a person can only mean one of two things: total annihilation, or a person that perdures.

Our nature as finite creatures comes to an end. Death *is* an annihilation in its biological aspect, but it is also a consummation of our personal aspect. What the good race of the middle years, the good works of self-actualization and psychic maturation are preparing us for is an encounter with judgment and eternity. Far from being negative, judgment is another mercy of God. Without it there would be no separation of good and evil,

141

no resolution of the ambiguities that characterize time, no dismissal of death and injustice as intermediary things.

The Catholic Church teaches that there will be both a particular and a general judgment. In the particular judgment, Jesus will evaluate each of us as unique individuals according to our faith, hope, love, and moral witness. Preparation for this gives meaning and purpose during our lives and for our deaths. At the end of time, there will be a second coming of Christ, and he will judge the living and the dead. This is the *general* judgment because it affects all people, and the *last* judgment because it terminates the history of the world.

In death, who we are as humans becomes transparent: by our very nature we are hard-wired for communion with God. All desires but one can fail: the desire to be loved, absolutely and unconditionally, a possibility that can only be realized in God. So what is our hope? That we will fall through death into the love of God and that this will be enough for us. Our hope finally rests in God.

Everything Leans to the Light

In his book *Small Graces*, Kent Nerburn relates how a Jesuit friend of his opened his heart to the beauty of gardens. His friend was a deeply learned man who spoke many languages and who had earned several advanced degrees, spending his life in the pursuit of ultimate issues: Who is God? What is the nature of good and evil? What is the meaning of life? But as he grew older, he turned his attention to the creation of a Japanese garden. The time he spent in his garden gradually exceeded the time he spent with his books. There, on his knees, day after day he would lovingly pluck a leaf, bend a twig, place a stone, or trim a branch until a shaft of light reached some leaf or stem with a rich and private life that no one noticed. When someone came to visit, he would point to a sliver of sunlight beaming down upon a small branch and draw attention to how it was turning to the light. He recounted how he had opened it to the sun last year, and how it took months, but that it slowly began turning its face toward the light.[1]

Life, death, and afterlife all come together in the intimacy of a garden's space. Everything lives. Everything dies. Everything leans to the light. If we knew only this, it would be enough.

You and I may not have a garden, but there are other ways, as expressed in this poem, of becoming aware of how "everything leans to the light."

The Quality of Light

Few things I hold more dear
than the quality of light
whose many moods by day
become more precious in the night.

Flowing silently through glass
its golden rays exude
a sense of gentle peace
and inner quietude.

At daybreak it summons forth
new hope for human hearts,
as to a window we find our way
to becalm our fits and starts.

In the midday sky it permeates
the clouds, so luminous and bright,
and even the shades of blue are changed
with the angle of the light.

If the vertical glare of three-o'clock
—the heart of day to strengthen—
is too direct, then wait: for all looks
different when soon the shadows lengthen.

At sunset it gloriously colors
the fringes of the clouds,
then wanes with light our energy
as night the day enshrouds.

Such is the power of light
that at the end of day
the wind and waves go with it
and growing things there stay.

And when in the middle of the night
we wake and check the time,
it's invariably with the question
"How long before the sun will shine?"

And if, even for a short span of days
its golden aura disappears,
we find our feelings and
our thoughts in serious arrears.

There's a truth revealed here
to be never lost from sight,
that at the end of all our days
we're meant to pass from light to Light.

A Parable

Our difficulty with the great questions of life and death is that we usually see them from one side only: light or dark. And where death is concerned, we tend to see only the dark side, the negative things that death actually does, while the other half of the circle—life after death—goes wanting because we cannot see that. That's natural enough because we're creatures who learn from what we can see, smell, taste, touch, and feel. So when we try to imagine something we have no experience of, we automatically invoke images based upon what we've experienced through our senses. It's hard for us to imagine and believe in a reality that's beyond our present one. How can we imagine the unimaginable? How can we picture the resurrection and life everlasting when none of us who are here alive has experienced it?

Our words about the life after death, like words about God, are necessarily analogical: partly the same, partly different. They are neither nonsense nor photographic reproductions, neither simple lies nor simple truths, but they are symbols, metaphors, images of the real thing.

One analogy that is particularly rich in giving us an idea of life after death is, ironically, birth. If we could talk to a baby in the womb and tell it of its unity with the mother, of how its pulse is one with the mother's pulse, and how it is living within and buoyed up by the waters in this secure place called the womb; if we could tell it that life in this place was about to end and that it was going to be expelled from the womb, pushed through a narrow passage, and that the cord that held it to its mother was going to be cut and that it would be on its own—well, if that baby could talk, it would probably say to us: "I'm going to die!"

There is a parable that employs this analogy, and though it risks being painful to women who have lost a child, our context here as a reflection on the afterlife makes it worth the telling.

Once upon a time, twin boys were conceived in the same womb. Seconds, minutes, hours passed as the two dormant lives developed. The spark of life glowed until it was fanned into fire with the formation of their embryonic brains. With their simple brains came feeling, and with feeling, perception—a perception of surroundings, of each other, of self.

When they perceived the life of each other and their own life, they knew that life was good, and they laughed and rejoiced. "Lucky are we to have been conceived and to have this world. Blessed is the Mother who gave us this life and each other."

Each budded and grew arms and fingers, lean legs and stubby toes. They stretched their lungs, churned and turned in their newfound world. They explored their world and found in it the life cord, which gave them life from the precious Mother's blood. So they sang, "How great is the love of the Mother that she shares all she has with us!" And they were pleased and satisfied with their lot.

Weeks passed into months, and with the advent of each new month, they noticed a change in each other and each began to see a change in himself. "We are changing," said the one. "What can it mean?"

"It means," replied the other, "we are drawing near to birth." An unsettling chill crept over the two and they both feared, for they knew that birth meant leaving their entire world behind. Said the one, "Were it up to me, I would live here forever."

"But we must be born," said the other. "It has happened to all the others who were here." For indeed there was evidence of life there before, as the Mother had borne others. "But mightn't there be life after birth?"

"How can there be life after birth?" cried the one. "Do we not shed our life cord and also the blood tissues? And have you ever talked to one who has been born? Has anyone ever reentered the womb after birth? No!"

He fell into despair and in his despair he moaned, "If the only purpose of our conception and all of our growth is that it be ended at birth, then truly our life is absurd."

"But there must be a Mother," protested the other. "Otherwise, who gave us our nourishment and our world?"

"We get our own nourishment and our world has always been here. And if there is a Mother, where is she? Have you ever seen her? Does she ever talk to you? No! We invented the Mother because it satisfied a need in us. It made us feel secure and happy."

So while the one raved and despaired, the other resigned himself to birth and placed his trust in the hands of his Mother. Hours ached into days and fell into weeks. And it came time. Both knew that their birth was close at hand, and both feared what they did not know.

As they were expelled from the womb, they cried and coughed out fluid and gasped the dry air. And when they were sure they had been born, they opened their eyes, seeing for the first time, and found themselves cradled in the warm, loving arms of their Mother.

They lay open-mouthed, awestruck before a beauty and truth they could not have hoped to either know or imagine![2]

Can you relate to the child who, never having experienced life outside the womb, had trouble believing in it; who hung on for dear life to what was known, to the life and routines within the womb, and who feared anything that threatened it?

Or perhaps you identified with the one who found it natural to believe in life after birth. Both babies were pleased and satisfied with their lot, but as they began to experience changes (aging), they interpreted their experience differently. Maybe each of those children voiced fears and hopes that you have felt at different times within yourself about the end of life as you know it.

In many ways, we are like those babies in the womb fearing birth. Our present world, for all its grandeur and all the opportunities it offers, could also be looked upon as a womb—bigger than our mother's, to be sure, but ultimately still small and constricting in terms of its potential to offer full and eternal life. And we're still being gestated (except now we call it aging), and the day is coming when a new pelvic thrust (death) will push us through a dim passage into a new world, and we won't have much to say about it. We'll have to trust that being born into this new, unknown world is what's best for us.

When we look at this through the eyes of faith, we see that calling death a new birth is not an analogy. It's reality! It's not *like* a birth, it *is* a birth! We emerged from the wombs of our mothers into a fascinating and marvelous world, only to learn along the way that this is but a larger version of that womb experience and that we are still being gestated and readied for birth into an even larger and more amazing universe that will leave us openmouthed and awestruck before a beauty and truth and love we could not have hoped to know or ever imagine.[3]

We call this "new" birth" experience "resurrection." A closer look at what the Church teaches about resurrection yields inspiration for our living.

The Resurrection

The argument between the two babies in the womb as to whether there was life after birth is an honest one. We would be mistaken to think that in the time of Jesus bodily resurrection was easily accepted. Authoritative circles among the Jews of the period did look for resurrection from the dead, but at the end of the ages. At the same time, the Sadducees rejected any such hope of what the future would hold. Above all, for those educated in the culture of the Hellenistic world, the idea of a dead man rising again appeared as a folly since they regarded the body as the tomb of the soul and looked forward to liberation from it.

And when it came to Jesus' rising from the dead, it did not come like a brute slap in the face to his critics, a nonnegotiable fact that left skeptics with nothing to say. The resurrection didn't make a big splash. It was not some spectacular event that exploded into the world as the highlight on the evening news. It had the same dynamics as the incarnation itself: After he rose from the dead, Jesus was seen by some, but not by others. He was understood by some, but not by others. Some got his meaning and it changed their lives, others were indifferent to him, and still others understood what had happened, hardened their hearts against it, and tried to destroy its truth.[4]

In our time, the doctrine of reincarnation, or transmigration of the soul, is gaining widespread exposure in the various forums of East-West encounter. It is important to clearly identify how the teaching about reincarnation and that about the resurrection are characterized by some significant differences. First, there is the straightforward declaration of New Testament scripture that "it is appointed for mortals to die once, and after that [receive] the judgment" (Heb 9:27).

Second, the selective manner in which reincarnation is perceived by many Westerners misrepresents its understanding in the religion (Hinduism) from which the teaching originates. Whereas many Westerners employ it as a convenience ("There's just not enough time to do everything I want to do in one life-time"), in its original matrix reincarnation does not add to life but, rather, adds to suffering. It is not cause for consolation, but for fear. Reincarnation is a warning to humanity: "Be careful not to do evil because you will be reborn to expiate it!" It is like telling someone in prison who is about to finish serving his time, that his punishment has been extended and he must start all over. Similar to how Jews, Christians, and Muslims fear death, Hindus fear rebirth. Christianity has something quite different to offer in regard to the problem of death. It proclaims that "One has died for all" and that death has been defeated; it is no longer a precipice over which all must plunge, but rather a bridge to the other shore—eternity.[5]

Third, reincarnation accords no salvation to the body; it is only the soul that transmigrates through various incarnations until, at last, it is liberated. In Christian understanding, the human soul is a spirit that is meant to give life to a physical body and to exercise itself in a body. Without a body, the human spir-itual soul is metaphysically deficient. It gains knowledge through the exercise of reason from information obtained from the senses. Human intelligence is thus oriented toward life in a body. That is why a complete restoration of the soul calls for a body in and through which the soul may express itself. In some real but unimaginable way, our bodies, like that of Jesus, will be taken up and be part of our existence forever.

A Bodily Resurrection

The assertion of faith that Jesus rose *bodily* from the dead bears further development. Christian doctrine does not ask us to believe, for example, that the body of Jesus was merely resusci-tated—that he simply got back the same body that he had before. If the resurrection of the body were a return to our ordi-nary physical state (in the same way that modern medicine brings clinically dead bodies back to life), then it would not be possible to speak of the *transformation* of our earthly existence.

Jesus' friend Lazarus was brought back from the grave to his ordinary physical state; he was resuscitated. And then he had to go through living and dying all over again. But Jesus rose from the grave *transformed*, never again to undergo death. Had he merely been resuscitated, the disciples with whom he fell into step on the road to Emmaus (Luke 24:1–35) would have recognized him. And he would not have had the freedom of movement indicated by the resurrection narrative that describes his sudden appearance in a locked room filled with frightened disciples (John 20:19–29).

At the same time, Jesus does not appear to have had a totally new or completely different type of body, nor was he merely a spirit or a ghost. He invited the disciples to examine the wounds in his hands and side (Luke 24:39), and to eat breakfast with him (John 21:9–12). The empty tomb pointed to the bodiliness of his resurrection. But what kind of body? He is the same as regards his *identity*, but he is clearly no longer the same as regards his *reality*. If we shall be like him, our resurrected bodies will be in mysterious continuity with what we have lived in our earthly bodies, and yet different, no longer subject to the limitations of time and space, sickness and aging and death.

According to the apostle Paul, what is involved in our own death and resurrection is neither a process of complete annihilation followed by a new creation, nor a process by which the dead body is simply restored to life. What resurrection entails is the redemption of our bodies, which signifies much more than a mere escape from suffering and death. It means the transformation of the whole material, bodily world with all that it contains of pain and suffering.

Paul uses the term *spirit-body* to characterize the risen body as one that is no longer restricted to an earthly mode of existence but is created anew in a "body of his glory" (Phil 3:21). There is no concept of duality here wherein spirit is immortal and matter is perishable. Christians believe that by becoming human, God endorsed the value of earthly realities. Our flesh is good and redeemed and not something sordid or evil that we need to escape.

Implications for Our Lives Now

As in all our reflections thus far, we want to continually keep in front of ourselves the very real implications within these themes for our *living* here and now. Remember to live! So what are the implications of a bodily resurrection for our living the life we have now?

We will respect our body and treat it well through right eating, regular exercise, and adequate rest. Since it is not simply that we *have* bodies but that we are rooted in our bodies and will always be so, all the dimensions of our lives—like working and playing, relaxing and love-making—are part of our spirituality. We submit all of them to the influence of the Spirit of God. In short, we go to God the way God came to us: in and through a body.

Resurrection is a teaching about the meaning and fate of the human body. What God did for Jesus, God plans to do for us. The doctrine of the resurrection says that the body itself is not a product, not a consumable. Though "biodegradable," it is not disposable. Though it may be broken, flawed, or worn out, each human body continues to be precious to its designer. God plans to keep the whole thing, the whole me. Christians "teach" resurrection by devising ways of life that care for human bodies.

So we will also carry an active concern for the physical needs of others in working to eradicate poverty, hunger, sickness, and violence. Jesus' resurrection was not an isolated event; he did not rise from the dead for himself alone. Were that the understanding, we would not be talking about it now with reference to ourselves. Paul's teaching on this is very clear: in baptism we are crucified and buried with Jesus (Rom 6:4–6). We live with him (6:8). We are heirs with him and are glorified with him (8:17). And our bodies will be changed to become like his glorious body (Phil 3:21). Though it may be difficult for us to think about it in anything but individualistic terms, if we wish to remain faithful to the biblical testimony, we must not separate the destiny of the individual from that of the community and of the entire created order.

Newness of Life

One could ask: What is the point of the resurrection? The answer, I think, is twofold, and the first part of the answer is "to elicit faith and bring us to newness of life." We need to be clear about the significance of this event. With the resurrection, we are dealing not with *a* question but *the* question of Christian faith. It is the founding event of the Church. Without it, there would have been no Christian faith and no Church. Paul laid it on the line to the Corinthians:

> If Christ has not been raised, then our proclamation has been in vain and your faith has been in vain....If Christ has not been raised, your faith is futile and you are still in your sins. Then those also who have died in Christ have perished. If for this life only we have hoped in Christ, we are of all people most to be pitied.
> (1 Cor 15:14, 17–19)

In raising Jesus from the dead, God did something new and unpredictable, without precedent in the whole span of human history before or after Jesus.

Did the resurrection elicit faith? The reaction of the apostle Thomas in encountering the risen Lord—"My Lord and my God!"—provides an affirmative response. But a statement of belief is not enough. The resurrection is not merely an object of faith, the acceptance of a theological truth. It is a *call to newness of life*. If we haven't been raised to newness of life by our faith in the resurrection, then it has not reached its intended aim. The great Easter truth is not that we are to live anew after death, but that we are to live anew *now* because of our experience of Christ's continued, empowering presence through the Holy Spirit. The life to come is not only a *hereafter*, but a *here-now*.

"What's the point of the resurrection?" The second part of the answer to this question is "for the liberation and salvation of the world." God wants to liberate all creation from oppression and estrangement. God wants to change people and to shape history through acts of love and forgiveness.

So, if faith is to bring us to newness of life, and the liberation and salvation of the world amounts to changing people and making things new, the question for us is: What's new? And what might this newness look like? How might we not merely *extend* but *exalt* our present existence? Here are some examples of how this newness of life might manifest:

This newness of life might look like parents forgiving themselves for having done a poor job of raising a child. It is their every effort now to love that child as best they can, accepting and loving themselves with all their limitations in the process.

This newness of life might look like a couple overcoming the doldrums of a plateaued relationship by risking new heart-to-heart communication with one another about that for which each longs.

This newness of life might look like an employee working up the courage to confront and expose policies in the workplace long felt to be unjust, or an overscheduled person learning to say "no" in order to create some personal space in which to breathe, to reflect, to *live*.

This newness of life is our release from behind the locked doors of burdening guilt, stunting self-recrimination, low self-esteem, and downward spiral of despair. It is the discovery that we are loved in spite of our failures. It is the rebirth of laughter, the creative imagining of new possibilities for our future.

The Spirit that has been bestowed upon us is not dormant within us, but is already in this present time actually bringing about that inner transformation that is intended to lead up to the glory that lies in the future. The empty tomb and the appearance stories in the scriptures tell us less about what happened to Jesus and more about what happened to his followers then and is happening to us now. They are essentially stories of conversion, stories that tell us about liberation and empowerment, about our reason for hope and for forgiveness. Jesus' immediate followers were changed from a demoralized group of fearful people in hiding into a group of enthusiastic witnesses who were willing to risk everything for him.

When the experience of Jesus' disciples becomes our own, then our life stories become like their life stories. In the end, the experience of Jesus' continued empowering presence transforms an old story into a contemporary one.

In our daily efforts to be responsive to the inner movement of the transforming Holy Spirit, it is critical that we be aware that we are not alone on this path to ever-deepening life. That assurance is given to us in what the Church calls "the Communion of Saints."

The Communion of Saints

The Communion of Saints is the Church, and there is more to the Church than we see here on earth. All believers, living and dead, form one body. This is the concept of "the Body of Christ" first described by Paul (Rom 12:4–8). Paul wanted us to understand that we are intimately related to Jesus and to one another. He explained that the Church functions like a human body: all the parts (members) unite toward the purpose of keeping the body alive and healthy. "If one member suffers, all suffer together. If one member is honored, all rejoice together. Now you are the body of Christ, individually members of it" (1 Cor 12:26–27).

Part of our Christian faith, as canonized in our creed, is the belief that our unity and community with each other in Christ is so real, so deep, so physical, and so mutually interdependent that we constitute not an aggregate or a corporation but an organism, a living body. The Body of Christ is a body in the way that a man or a woman is a body. The unity inside that body is not mystical or analogical: it's real. What happens for health or for disease in any one cell, be it ever so small, eventually affects the health of the whole body.

All the parts of the Body of Christ are connected. In this solidarity, the least of our acts done in charity redounds to the benefit of all. Similarly, every sin harms this communion. The outcome of every private moral battle will impact upon it. There is no such thing as a "private" sin or a "private" good act. Since all the faithful form one body, the good of each is communicated to the others. In short, there is both a communion among persons and a communion of goods in the Church. The riches of Christ are communicated to all the members through the sacraments. And as the Church is governed by one and the same Spirit, all the goods it has received become a common fund. The Communion of Saints is a belief in spiritual aid.

The Church We Do Not See

The Church we see is only a small part of the whole Church. There are those who have completed their earthly lives and who are now fully in the presence of God, gazing with unveiled face on the glory of the Lord. These saints are to God like stained glass is to sunlight. Light from the sun is white, but when it passes through the prism of many different lives, it shows itself in varied and glorious hues. God's glory is reflected in the saints.

In honoring the saints in heaven, it is not just the great and famous names that we remember, but all the baptized. A saint refers to anyone who is in union with Christ, not just to those who have been canonized saints. The Communion of Saints includes our deceased parents and grandparents, teachers, friends, and colleagues who have been saints in our own lives. And it also includes those millions of the baptized whom we cannot name, who are not known to us, but who have served God faithfully in their own way, time, and place. This is the Church we do not see. Those who make it up are like a cheering section for those in the Church on earth who are still on pilgrimage.

All of us, in varying degrees and in different ways, share in the same love toward God and our neighbors. Our union with one another is reinforced by an exchange of spiritual goods. Those more closely united to Christ in heaven help in many ways to build up the Church on earth. I think of the saints in heaven like a vast crowd filling a stadium, yelling their support and cheering on those of us who are still on the playing field sweating and trying to move the ball forward.

The Church We See

Belief in the Communion of Saints makes clear that to be baptized is not a private act between God and the solitary individual. It is to be a member of the "holy catholic Church" and the Communion of Saints, as the Apostles' Creed reminds us. In the current secular, Western culture of individualism and privatism, to celebrate the Communion of Saints is a countercultural act.

For those in the Church on earth, the most natural way to celebrate the Communion of Saints is around the table of the Eucharist. The Eucharist is the feast of all the saints in heaven and on earth, the place where we join with the famous ones, the dear ones, the unknown ones. The various commemorations of the saints in the liturgical calendars of some Church traditions are like signposts along the road to the reign of God. Among Eastern Christians, church buildings came to be filled with icons, images of the saints, which served as visual reminders of the great communion to which we all belong.

Christianity, like almost all world religions, recognizes the need for growth and purification before our salvation is complete. Jesus taught us to use our talents to advance God's reign on earth by living lives of love and service. But most of us fall short of this ideal because of ego-centeredness. Our unloving, ego-centered self needs to be transformed into a God-centered, loving self, and that project is always a work in progress.

How this purifying process of dying to oneself in order to rise with Christ takes place, and whether it happens in the course of this life or after, we do not know. But we recognize that all those who are involved in the process are also part of the Communion of Saints. We are all on the way toward that fullness of life that God intends for us. The good news is that, through his resurrection, Jesus revealed to us that death is only a checkpoint to be passed. In crossing that line or going through that door, we go from one part of the Communion of Saints to another.

Prayer With and For One Another

While we are on earth, those who have gone before us and who were close to us in life, who gave us inspiration, strength, comfort, and loving support, continue to do so in the afterlife. They continue to share a spiritual bond with us in the Body of Christ even after death. When we pray with and for those who have died, we are strengthening and deepening these spiritual relationships. There are some wonderful testimonies to this conviction of faith, like the inscription composed by St. Seraphim of Sarov for his tombstone:

> When I am dead, come to me at my grave, and the more often the better. Whatever is on your soul, whatever may have happened to you, come to me as when I was alive and, kneeling on the ground, cast all your bitterness upon my grave. Tell me everything and I shall listen to you, and all the bitterness will fly away from you. And as you spoke to me when I was alive, do so now. For I am living, and I shall be forever.[6]

Often when life is difficult for us, we ask a relative or close friend to pray for us. We can ask the same of those who have gone before us "since we are surrounded by so great a cloud of witnesses," as the Letter to the Hebrews says (12:1). They have died in God's favor and now stand before God face to face. They are more alive than us, more aware of happenings on earth—desirous of aiding us, and able to be asked for help and to assist us with their prayer and their intercession, as described in this scene in the Book of Revelation: "Another angel with a golden censer came and stood at the altar; he was given a great quantity of incense to offer with the prayers of all the saints on the golden altar that is before the throne. And the smoke of the incense, with the prayers of the saints, rose before God from the hand of the angel" (Rev 8:3).

Unfinished Business

To believe in the Communion of Saints is to believe that those who have died are still alive and are connected with us in such a way that we can continue to talk with them and that our relationship with them can continue to grow. This is important because too often we have unfinished business with the deceased.

We loved each other, but as with all families, there were areas of tension. Even inside our most intimate relationships, there are shadows of resistance, some irritations, maybe even some negative feelings. There is no such thing in this life as clearcut, pure love. In every relationship there are experiences of disappointment, of boredom, of being misunderstood, of not being properly valued, of being wounded.

A death in which someone dies cradled in the loving arms of family, friends, and Church, fully at peace with God and everyone, is perhaps a hoped-for scenario. But the reality is that oftentimes death comes with an unexpected suddenness, by accident, by contingency, or with a seeming randomness, as when someone is hit by a drunken driver, or dies from drug overdose, suicide, or massive heart attack.

When that happens, there is no time to say we're sorry, to ask for forgiveness, to do the things we should have done, or to say goodbye. Perhaps we had hurt or been hurt by the person, or are left feeling remorse because we weren't as available as we wanted to be, too busy with our own lives. And now it's too late. Death has separated us and there are some important things left unresolved. So we find ourselves sitting under a cloud of guilt and regret, needing reconciliation, needing resolution, needing more time.

And the good news is that there *is* more time—on both sides—for reconciliation and for healing. Inside the Communion of Saints we have privileged access to each other and there we can finally speak all of those words that we couldn't speak before. We can reach across death's divide. When Jesus says to the good thief on the cross, "This day you will be with me in paradise," his words are meant for everyone of us who dies without yet fully being a saint and without having had the time and opportunity to make all the amends we would like to make.[7]

And as for those of us who are left behind, this is where prayer for the dead comes in. Prayer's first effect is always in *us*. It is impossible to pray consistently for something without being changed from within by our own prayer. So the first reason we pray for the dead is that it helps and consoles us, the living. Second, we pray for our deceased loved ones to help heal our relationship with them. Praying for that person helps wash clean those things that remain painful between us. Within the Communion of Saints, the connection is purer, the forgiveness deeper, and the distance between us lesser than even in our face-to-face conversations. And third, praying for the dead offers real strength and encouragement to them in the same way that a loving presence to each other offers strength and consolation here in this life. Whenever we move to a new place and context, there is some pain because we have not yet fully let go of where we were before. With our prayer, we offer encouragement to the deceased in their pain of letting go of their attachments in this life (classically called purgatory by Catholics) and in their efforts to adjust to a new life. As Ron Rolheiser writes:

> From my own experience of having loved ones die, as well as from what others have shared with me, I have found that usually, after a time, we sense that our deceased loved ones no longer need us to pray for them. Now they just want us to connect with them.
>
> Prayer for the dead does that and even though our prayers might still need to be formulated as if we are praying for them, we are simply connecting with them and what was formerly a cold, cutting absence now becomes a warm, comforting presence.[8]

When Christians pray in the creed, "I believe in the Communion of Saints," we are postulating that our loved ones who have died are still in relationship with us and that this relationship continues to change and grow even after we are separated by death. What we can't bring to wholeness in this life can, if we take the Communion of Saints seriously, be completed afterward. We still have a privileged communication with our loved ones after death.

Finally, it is worth noting that the foundation of this Communion of Saints only came about through the actual death and resurrection of the Church's founder. This communion will undoubtedly include people from other religions whose holiness followed other patterns—like the Roman centurion (Matt 8:5–13) or the Canaanite woman (Matt 15:21–28), both of whose faith Jesus described as great even though they were not Jews—but whose lives reflected God's light. In its own way, the Communion of Saints demonstrates that there are marvelous developments on the other side of death.

I Watched a Cloud Dissolve

I watched a cloud dissolve today,
a spool of ragged fleece visibly spinning,
driven by the energy of the sun,
while others around it remained stable and serene.

Soon it snagged some wayward threads
on one more placid than itself
and began to flay apart, to unravel
before my eyes like a human disposition

which sometimes, too, enters our space
fluffy and soft or ominous and dark
but always capable of transformation,
of being gently pulled by others nearby

into another way of being.
Within minutes, as I watched,
it became something else.
We wield more influence than we know.

Resources for Your Inner Work

Reflections

1. Take a sheet of paper and write down the names of people who have died with whom you were close.
2. Is there some way in which you sense they continue to be with you, aware of you, in relationship to you? Are there particular times or places when this feeling comes through more strongly than at other times?
3. Write a few lines for each of those whose names are on your paper, expressing what you most appreciated about them.
4. Is there anything in particular for which you would like to ask them now?
5. Whom would you cite among your saints on earth here and now? Do you express your appreciation for their place in your life and the contribution they make?
6. Is your understanding of the Communion of Saints inclined more toward the saints in heaven (the Church we do not see) or toward the saints on earth? Do you ask for the intercession of both?

Prayer

Thank you, God,
for the promise of life eternal
with those who have died
in their mortal bodies
and risen with Christ
in their glorified bodies.
I think of them with you,
those whom I love and miss,
now enjoying your presence.
They know of my love for them,
and I of theirs for me.
Grant that their arms may be
among the first to embrace and
receive me into the life of heaven.

Greenwich Beach

I was *there*,
in the sweet spot of life!
The sand wet and firm
for low-tide meandering,
the sea in the sunlight
shiny and flat like a griddle,
the seagulls in graceful flight
daring me to swim out of sight.

And I *left it!*
Gave up the heart of the melon
for the rind,
for a road on a map,
for an idea in the mind.

And at the end of the day
the compulsion to cover ground
was unmasked in review,
and a judgment came down,
full of wisdom and ken,
to find ecstasy in the moment
and never look beyond it again.

Chapter Seven

Your Life Now

In these times of rapid sociological and technological transformation, nothing is more important than learning the skills of personal renewal.

—M. J. Ryan

Facing the realities of aging, illness, and death squarely, and accepting their inevitability, has a big reward. When we truly accept that life as we know it on this lovely green-and-blue planet is not given in limitless supply, we begin to think more clearly about what is important to us, what we want to do with the time we have, how we want to use our available resources, and how we want to employ the talents with which God has gifted us to both enjoy and leave our world better than we found it.

When we begin to engage with questions like these, the gap begins to close between what we *say* our priorities are and where our time and energy actually go. The trip we've been saying for years that is "high on our list" now becomes the plan for this year's vacation. The project dear to our hearts that's been sitting patiently in abeyance finally gets some time. Our resources cease gathering dust and begin making a difference in the lives of others.

There is a Sufi tale that speaks to the question:

Once upon a time many people gathered together in the marketplace to ask questions of the master. Some were seriously interested in the truth and in changing their lives to conform with the power of goodness and life that was the God they sought to know. Many came

164

out of curiosity or were dragged along by friends. Some just found themselves there. Some were intent on invalidating and tripping up the master because they served others and saw the master as a threat to their place in their own groups. And there were the master's own followers, who often didn't understand what was going on until long after the discussions were finished.

That day all the questions seemed to be about death, the grave, and whether one could be sure of a life after death. It was very disconcerting, especially to the master's own disciples, because in response to all the questions the master only laughed. Sometimes softly, a mere chuckle. Sometimes raucously, very undignified. Sometimes with pleasure. Sometimes almost convulsively. Those who asked and those who listened reacted with anger, confusion, a feeling of being insulted. But he spoke no words, just laughed. Finally, the master walked away from them all.

Later that night the disciples prodded him and demanded that he speak about the morning. What had he meant? They were really distraught and perplexed. He looked at them in mock seriousness and spoke: "Have you ever noticed who the people are who keep asking questions about the next life—life after death? It seems that all of them, for one reason or another, have trouble with this one. They always seem to want another life that isn't connected to this one much at all."

This didn't settle the disciples' anxiety, and one sputtered out: "But master, is there a life after death or not? Speak plainly. Say yes or no!" The master did it again: he laughed out loud. Then he asked a question back: "What I want to know," he said, "is whether there is life *before* death?" And he eyed them all. "Are any of you really alive?"[1]

Being Really Alive

What does it mean for each of us to be "really alive"? We know that we can have power and social status and money and still feel dead inside. We know that though our work can succeed, our quality of life can still decline. Sometimes our life balance, a source of contentment in itself, is overturned by our very successes. Our professional lives may be humming, but there are important inner aspirations that continue to be neglected. What will fan those glowing coals into flame until they rise up and dance?

Kevin taught high school English and religion, and coached cross-country and track-and-field for twenty-eight years. At fifty-two, he made another choice:

> Whenever I was asked why I became a teacher, I could never point to the specific moment of awareness of my teaching vocation, but I do know that its evolution within me was as natural as that of a human fetus within a mother's womb. Likewise, coaching was merely another form of teaching, adding another dimension to the way that I could relate to my students, a mutual deepening in understanding one another. I truly believe that I became what I was meant to be—for that time of my life.
>
> I loved both of the subject matters I taught and the sports I coached, and had discovered a tremendous passion within me for all of them, a passion that I unabashedly was able to share with my students and athletes in ways that evidently inspired interest and enthusiasm in them as well. Over the years, however, while my love for these areas remained strong, I felt my reservoir of energy for passionately sharing this love diminishing. Sure, I was getting older, and a mid-afternoon nap often sounded far more appealing to me than my daily run, but something more seemed at play here, as if the reservoir was not so much drying up as being slowly siphoned off to another area of my life thirsting for more time and energy.
>
> Generally, I am a "high bar" person. I don't do much of anything if I am not going to give it 100 or more percent effort. When I choose to do something, I choose to do it well

and with as much gusto as I can give it to help it succeed; and, of course, my sense of its "success" is not simply in completing the task—"to finish"—but to arrive at a respectable, even honorable, place. In some ways, I suppose, this idea of success both fueled and drained the energy of my efforts.

While I always enjoyed the sense of achievement, I was also keenly aware that each year as I placed high standards on all of my efforts, I was also agreeing to an inevitable load of stress that would annually manifest itself in physical aches, frequent illness, and, more than anything, a constant feeling of just being run-down. With an increasing awareness of the toll that my personal demands wreaked on my physical well-being, I thoughtfully explored different approaches to how and what I did. Yes, I could "lighten up" a bit, and did, but I could not compromise on the integrity of my doing my jobs well. In the last two years of my high school teaching and coaching career, however, I became more conscious of a shifting perspective in my idea of success.

Early in our "career lives," we obviously need a job to support our needs, and those of a growing family should we venture down that path; additionally, I do think that it is important that we seek to find gainful employment in areas that validate who and how we are. Most of our waking hours are spent at our job, and if I do not enjoy it or feel validated by it—the most fundamental measure of a job's "success"— I cannot help but believe that my other waking hours will also be infected by a kind of subconscious disdain for life itself, a gnawing unhappiness.

A job is certainly important in paying the bills and expenses of our lives, but if it does nothing more than provide an income, it will always and only be "work" with none of the potentially positive aspects of that word. For me, teaching and coaching had always been, truly, much more a vocation than a job or "work." And, fortunately, this vocation provided me numerous layers of success: enjoyment and validation; inspired and emerging writers, thinkers, and runners; words and awards of appreciation; moral victories; and state championships. All of these were good and wonderful in their time, but at fifty years old (and I don't believe because of my age), something was evidently changing within me. In a simple way of seeing it, familial, communal, and social successes had been achieved; what was asking for attention and energy now was something more personal.

Although it seems like a cliché, I do believe that much of our social, and even to some degree personal, sense of success and achievement is measured by financial stability and independence. As I was the sole financial provider for a growing family subsisting on my parochial school income (which generally meant about 70 percent of my public school colleagues' income), we pretty much lived "hand-to-mouth" for most years.

Then, each child slipped away into independent living, a second income was added, and suddenly life got much more comfortable and easy, at least with regard to financial concerns. I was enjoying the comfort, but that which was supplying the comfort, my vocation-job, was no longer providing me the same emotional and spiritual satisfaction. I knew that something had to change, but as the nation's economy nosedived into its worst slump since the depression and I daily read the tragic stories of ever-increasing unemployment and foreclosures, a "rational" shift in my life seemed inappropriate if not impossible. To make matters worse, continuing to carry the burden of my increasing lack of happiness seemed even more inappropriate and impossible.

I have always been a person of deep faith, the cultivation and nourishment of my spirituality being core components of my life, and this new emergence was nothing if it wasn't also spiritual. Personally and privately, I prayed and meditated over this new vine growing within and out of me. Meanwhile, socially, providential connections were made that seemed to provide the latticework upon which the vine could grow; and like all plant growth, unseen in its movement but evident in its leafing and flowering, I became very aware that the time had come for me "to jump." The whisper of words with which the Spirit chided me was, "If you dare to step outside your 'known room,' that place of comfort and security, I will provide." All my life, it seemed, I had privately and even publicly proclaimed a belief in a cosmic, spiritual energy that surrounds all life; now, if I truly believed in a larger-than-life vision, it seemed to me that my "day of reckoning" had arrived.

Having often quoted the words of the master teacher, Jesus of Nazareth, "Consider the lilies of the field and the birds of the air..." (Matt 6:28–35), I had already long weighed the financial implications of the move, looking at myself in an inner mirror asking, "Since when has money or comfort or security mattered so much to you, Kevin?" But the truth was, when I finally went public with my decision to resign from my teaching and coaching posts, more than anything, I feared a backlash of disdainful and negative responses— feared that people would interpret the move as nothing more than an economically ill-advised response to a midlife crisis. More than I cared to admit, along with the reasonable financial concerns, was my "social status" concern: how would I appear in the eyes of my colleagues, peers, and those of other social circles?

The first gift of my decision arrived as immediately as the announcement of my resignation itself; I was overwhelmed by the incredible support I received. While colleagues rued my exit on a professional level, all voiced excitement for my potential new horizons on a personal level. And most shocking of all, a response I had never anticipated, was a kind of jealousy or envy, not of the "deadly sin" nature, but one that indirectly gave voice to the inner yearnings in so many people. They, as I, knew that my action was not a "retirement," for I was too young. It was, rather, truly a letting go late in a career of a comfortable and known way of life, a letting go of "making a living," and opting for "whatever the Spirit might provide."

Sure, the inevitable question of "What are you going to do now?" was asked with frequency, but the only and indefinite answer I could give them seemed to only spark a deeper sense of desire in the questioner who would then muse, "I wish that I could do that."

They could do it, we all could, but for the same reasons with which I wrestled for years, we *feel* that we can't. And this is why my decision to "move on," the label with which I correct people who ask me about "my retirement," has been such a spiritual adventure, a veritable "leap of faith."

Feeling locked inside the social conventions into which we step as responsible adults, we believe that the key to the lock, if it is locked at all, has been thrown away or mislaid. We believe we now have no choice but to establish our lives within the limited space provided. And indeed, early on, with growing families and career decisions, pragmatically there are reasonable boundaries.

But as our life unfolds, so too should our options. What I realized, however, was that many more people than I ever imagined were dreamily looking out the windows of their limited space, assuming that there was no way out. A simple and unanticipated but great gift that I received was voiced by a parent of former students who, seeing my decision as a "model," told me with his somewhat envious accent, "Isn't it interesting that even as you leave teaching, you are still teaching?"

I don't share that reflection to boast of my decision, but to share my wonder in what has happened as well as my own growing awareness of the hunger that so many of us carry around privately within us, a hunger for something more. Not more *stuff*, but more meaning and satisfaction in knowing who we are and what we are truly capable of and are called to be.

Can You Drink the Cup?

We're never too old to make a new beginning, to open to fuller life. A friend, Suzanne, turned her life around in midstream seven years ago by giving up alcohol. "My sobriety date," she wrote, " just happens to be my son Zachary's birthday. I always tell him that I am younger than he is, as I now view December 7 as my real birthday—the day I truly became Suzanne. So he turned twenty-three and I turned seven!"

Accepting that she was addicted to alcohol was a kind of surrender for her. As people in the developed world, we receive good training in power and performance principles, but not much attention is given to letting go, to detachment, and certainly not to any kind of surrender. "Surrender" sounds like losing, and we do not like that. And yet, in the Christian faith, the clearest and most tangible expression we have of God is Jesus, who seems to be "losing" by every criteria imaginable. The message of the cross reframes surrender. Where once it looked like losing, now it looks like accessing a deeper, broader sense of the self that is already content and abundant. We might call it the "true self" or who-you-are-in-God. Once we move our identity to that level of deep inner contentment and draw life from that deeper Abundance, why would we ever again settle for a scarcity model of life, one that continually leaves us feeling, "This is not enough," or, "I'm not enough"? In God and in grace, we are overwhelmed by more-than-enough-ness! We come to understand that whatever we have is enough. And life itself becomes rich again. Nothing drives our reach to extend beyond our grasp. Nothing is left to us now but ourselves, held in the grace of God, and that is enough.

In the Gospel of Matthew, the mother of James and John, two of the disciples, made a rather extraordinary request of Jesus. She asked him to promise that her sons would have places of honor in his kingdom, one at his right hand and the other at his left. Jesus' answer was, "You do not know what you are asking. Are you able to drink the cup that I am about to drink?" (20:22).

When Henri Nouwen resigned from his prestigious chaplaincy position at Yale University, he went to live at L'Arche Daybreak in Toronto, Canada, a community of people whose core members are those with mental disabilities. Henri reflected that the question Jesus asked went right to the heart of his own life as a human being, of his priesthood. When, as a young priest, he had held the beautiful golden chalice of the Mass in his hands, that question didn't seem hard to answer. He was a newly ordained priest, full of ideas and ideals. Life seemed to be rich with promise. He was eager to drink the cup!

But there came a day when he was celebrating Mass with about twenty members of the Daybreak community in a small basement chapel and the story was read in which Jesus raises that question. Suddenly, Henri reflected, the words "Can you drink the cup?" pierced his heart like the sharp spear of a hunter. He knew at that moment—as with a flash of insight—that taking this question seriously would radically change his life.

"Can you drink the cup?" It is the question that has the power to crack open hearts fed on ambition and desire for status and take life's meaning to a deeper level. Can you drink the cup? Can you empty it to the dregs? Can you taste all the sorrows and joys? Can you live your life to the full whatever it will bring? These are our questions.[2]

Mary Claire, a wife, mother, and grandmother in her late fifties, reflects on the shape of those questions in her life:

Several very significant events in my life have made me look at what is important. My younger sister Ann was born blind and epileptic, and with severe mental disabilities. My parents chose to raise her at home rather than institutionalize her. She was part of our family and went everywhere with us regardless of others' reaction to her. We learned responsibility early in caring for her as well as being open to those that are "different" from the norm. Because of Ann, my volunteer and advocacy career path was a natural one. She died at age thirty-five.

My oldest brother, Gary, died suddenly at age thirty-five as well. We expected Ann to die earlier rather than later, but not Gary, a husband, a father of three. His autopsy revealed a massive and fast-growing brain tumor. Sitting in the hospital chapel, my anger boiled over and I kept asking God why. These experiences made me want to live life as fully as possible, and I proceeded to live it intensely. After a few years it became clear I needed to find a better balance. The intensity was leading to burnout. Balance became my constant challenge and focus, and the more I managed to strike one, the better things were. Life was going along well.

Then came a piece of news that caused me to fall off my balance beam. "You have breast cancer," my doctor told me. Cancer is entirely different from any other challenge or loss that I had experienced in my life previously. This time there was no asking why because I knew there wasn't any answer. The oncologist said I was in "perfect" health other than breast cancer. My own body had betrayed me.

One of my coping mechanisms in life has been being physically active. Running, wilderness canoe trips, and skiing, be it water, cross-country, or downhill. Now all of that and my life as I knew it changed. Now it was time to follow a new game plan, which included surgery, radiation, and drug therapy. A plan that keeps changing. How to find balance again? I tell God I want to recover a normal life, all the while knowing it will be a different "normal."

The battle to get to that new normal is difficult and not over yet. Going to bed at 5:30 p.m. is common. At this summer's 10-kilometer run for cancer research, instead of running, I walked it. Friends wore hats that said "Cancer Sucks" and walked with me. Dealing with side effects of medication is ongoing. A lot of my time is spent with the physical therapist and lymphedema specialist. Commitments and activities have to be streamlined in order to focus on getting healthy. Deliberate decisions have to be made whether to hold on to my Nordic-skiing coaching position and my downhill-skiing instruction program. In the summer, energy is saved for early morning waterskiing sessions with my son. Everyday tasks are put aside when my granddaughter wants to make muffins or to play at the lake with me.

Life just got a lot "shorter" when cancer entered the picture. So what will I do with today? Handle the necessary tasks of daily living and be glad that I can. Focus on the jobs I have chosen. Work at getting healthy (and yes—it is work!). Appreciate the beautiful surroundings that I live in. Enjoy the family and friends that are part of my life. Now I live more in the present, and let go of the things I have no control over. I am not recommending getting cancer as a way to help prioritize your life. But the good that has come out of a bad diagnosis is reorganizing my life and helping me to remember to *live*.

Mary Claire has chosen to "drink the cup," to empty it to the dregs, with all its sorrows and joys. What is in your cup and what is in mine are going to be different, but the question is the same: Do we choose to drink it and to taste every drop? Can we live in the same fullness with which Nature dies?

O But to Live as Nature Dies!

O but to live as nature dies—
with luminous expression
and phosphorescent bursts of being!

To flow with the energy of one's calling
like the glaciers of gold and orange
that swirl down mountain valleys.

To warm oneself with the heat of love
like the cone-shaped evergreen chimneys
surround themselves with the burning coals of molten maples.

To exude a joy in living
like a grove of yellow aspen exploding
in a mushrooming cloud of radiant light.

To rejoice in the diversity of peoples and cultures
as in the painter's pallette of colors
generously splotched upon the hillsides.

O but to live as nature dies—
with such liberality of being to soften the end
as autumn does with winter.

"How to find balance again?" Mary Claire asks. It's an
ongoing question for us all, as the fine-tuning dial in our living
seldom seems to hold a clear signal for long and constantly
needs to be readjusted. It's a key spiritual life question, "spiritual
life" here understood in a thoroughly holistic way, as encom-
passing all the aspects of our lives. Continuing growth and
development is the name of the game. Our lives are an ongoing
process. Kevin will continue to look at the question of what is
the best course for his life personally and professionally. Mary
Claire will keep climbing up on her balance beam, and when
she falls off, she'll get back up and restabilize herself.

The balancing postures in yoga are among the most challenging. When you are standing on one leg, you may look more
stable than you feel. The onlooker may see poise and stability,
but you are aware of the muscles twitching in your feet and legs,
struggling to maintain the posture. Finding and holding balance
in our living is similar. It involves subtle movements and shifts,
stretching and straining, constant adjustment, persevering effort,
patience and self-compassion, and a good sense of humor.

Finding the balance in our living will look different from one
person to the next, depending on our life situation. In the period
following her surgery and chemotherapy treatments for ovarian
cancer, Gwendolyn shared what balance looked like in her life:

The lesson of balance is not an easy one to learn, certainly
not for me, a "doer" if there ever was one. Taking time to
simply "be" is not something I easily allow myself. I've always

been driven to do all the practical things that "need" doing before I take the time for those much more life-giving activities that are creative or bring me joy. Now, at long last, I am learning to change how I prioritize my daily activities. So far I haven't much energy for things like singing, playing the piano or guitar, or taking photographs. Instead, I read, write, listen to music, walk, swing in the park, do my other exercises, and sit quietly drinking in the sunshine and the beauty of nature. When I have both time and energy, there are outings, films, and friends to see.

The most important thing, I believe, is to simply live as fully as possible in the moment, whatever happens. Even if I were dying, it would still be important to live as fully as possible until I die. I know it's not popular or even comfortable for a lot of people to talk about death but it's real and will happen to us all. Having faced it square-on, I'm stronger, more sure of who I am, of who God is, of my faith, and of what I want to do with the rest of my life.

In talking about balance in our living, we're essentially talking about how we hold ourselves open to the grace of God in the changing circumstances of our lives, and how we can give concrete expression to it in the hours of what for us is a normal day.

For monks and others who have a very structured and organized rhythm to their lives, the question will be differently posed: How can my routine remain life-giving for me and not simply become an unthinking pattern that leads to a colorless plateau? As a friend in her fifties wrote on the occasion of her birthday: "My life is relatively well organized and reflects my choices and priorities. But at the same time, I feel the risk of 'habit,' comfortable and secure habits that do not require me to take many risks toward something new and different."

The paschal mystery is always inviting us to open our hands and hearts to this new, fresh moment of life, to new people and places, new ways of looking at old questions. The conviction that every new experience of life only comes through an experience of letting go gives us courage to face Kevin's question and to respond with faith and trust, as he did, to the voice heard within: "If you dare to step outside your 'known room,' that place of comfort and security, I will provide."

Creative Aging

The gift hidden in aging is discovering that life is more than accomplishment. Once we have had some experience of success in our line of work, we are ready to look beyond that for more meaning. We are ready to move from success to significance. As the journey outward begins to slow down, the journey inward can pick up. Creative aging depends on reclaiming those parts of ourselves that we have relegated to the margins of our existence because of the unrelenting intensity of other demands upon us. The challenge now is to consciously pursue generativity rather than simply putting in time; not just to "give back" but to "give forward," making the world in which we live and work better than we found it. It involves a choice. As we gradually have more time and energy to spend on exploration and discovery, where we will invest it? Is endless leisure the reward for our striving, or will we look for more?

In her book *Creative Aging*, Marjory Zoet Bankson observes that one of the marks of aging in a generative way is offering ourselves for some larger purpose rather than simply protecting what we have. She points out that never before have so many North Americans reached retirement age with such advanced education, social consciousness, and good health. What will we do with it? We have an unprecedented opportunity to learn, to grow, and to offer our unique gifts to our neighborhood or city, to a school or health care facility. With the increasingly tentative financial scene, there is additional impetus to create new patterns of work, to explore part-time employment as well as volunteer service. We can either spend our lives in regret, bemoaning what we may have lost, or we can face the future with hope and curiosity, remembering that creativity is part of our nature.[3]

While stretching our financial resources to cover the years ahead, can we find a healthy and life-giving balance between enjoying some of the opportunities afforded by a more leisurely lifestyle, and actively engaging in community service and spiritual discovery? In striking that balance, we will likely find ourselves more alive and joyful than we have ever been. Isaac

Hecker, the founder of the Paulist Fathers, once made a striking statement. "My best years," he said, "have always been the present ones."[4] What would it take for us to be able to honestly say the same in this present season of our lives?

Resources for Your Inner Work

Reflections

Kevin's reflection on his life and work gives us a handle on several questions for ourselves.

1. He writes how, over the years, his passion and interest for the areas of his work diminished, but he recognized that it was not so much a case of "drying up as one of being slowly siphoned off to another area of my life thirsting for more time and energy." Does this observation find any traction in your own life?
2. Concerning the work we do, he writes that the most fundamental measure of a job's "success" is the extent to which we enjoy it and feel validated by it, and that if the rating here is low, other waking hours will be infected by "a gnawing unhappiness." Do you agree? Do you both enjoy and feel validated by your work? If not, are you aware of a "gnawing unhappiness"? What options do you have to move toward something more life-giving for you at this stage of your life?
3. Kevin wrote: "The whisper of words with which the Spirit chided me was, 'If you dare to step outside your "known room," that place of comfort and security, I will provide.'" Do you believe there is a divine Providence that guides our journey and provides us with what we need along the way?

Exercise on Finding Balance

Mary Claire was focused on living a life balanced between family and work, playing and praying, developing personally and serving the needs of others even before her diagnosis of breast cancer. Her struggle for balance only continued in new circumstances.

Finding balance usually means juggling such key aspects as our primary relationships, support system of friends and community, spiritual attunement, food and eating, work and prosperity, fun and recreation, physical well-being, and personal development and creativity. Using the Wheel of Life below, assess your own current life balance.

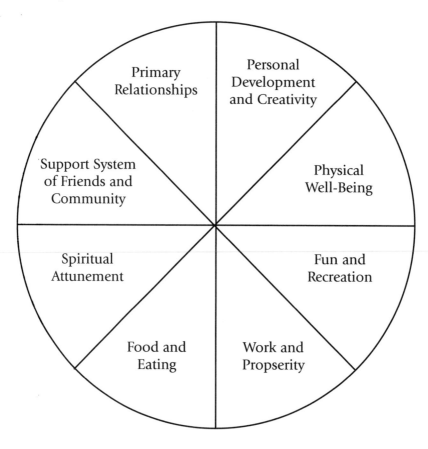

Wheel of Life

1. Evaluate each key aspect of your life according to your current level of satisfaction with each. In an honest assessment, write a number from 1 to 10 in each segment of the wheel, with 1 being low and 10 being high.

2. Now observe how much of the wheel is out of balance. If it were a tire, where is it "flat," where does it need more "air"?
3. Write a paragraph describing in as much detail as possible how you think you might improve the balance and quality of your life.
4. Finally, share your observations with someone and ask for their support as you seek to make some adjustments.

Poem

Sunset

Go.
Put down the book.
Open the door and step outside.
This sunset will last only a few moments.
In these clouds your life and whole world are reflected.
This golden fleece curled about the mountain
asks you to open your soul
to be all here
now.

Soon
this radiant glow
like all we love will be pulled beyond
our tenacious grasping in the flow of time.
The only answer is to open your heart to it fully,
to let your eyes fill with tears of tenderness
at the dizzying, knee-buckling beauty
delivered all unordered for your
awakening.

Cloud-color
unfolds moment to moment
like every state of mind dissolves
into another hearing, seeing, tasting, touching
until the breath you're breathing now will end.
Nothing stays the same and there's no solid ground

beneath your feet save for
the insecure security of
faith.

Prayer

My God.
I have feared joy.
I have held back from
the fullness of life,
bound by invisible threads
of old loyalties.
I have imagined that you
begrudged me my joy and fulfillment,
that you would intentionally
disrupt my happiness,
stifle my freedom,
rein in my delight.
Now I see that you
have always been calling me forth
like Lazarus from the tomb:
"Untie him and let him go!"
You desire the fullness of
life for me,
abundant, overflowing.
Unbind me, free me for joy,
That I may be fully alive.
You have held nothing back from me.
Help me to hold nothing
back in this life,
to live it to the fullest,
to drink deeply of joy—
your joy which you desire
to share with me forever.

—*Phillip Bennett*[5]

You

The Buddha said that receiving a human birth
is more rare than the chance that a blind turtle
floating in the ocean would stick his head through
   a small hoop.

So how will you practice gratitude today?
How seize the grace of conscious life,
how celebrate a mind that can know
   "This moment is like this"?

You poked your head through the hoop,
found the hole in the ice and surfaced. You
are given this short, precious time to know life
firsthand, to have your own experience. You
                  get the privilege.
                     You.

Chapter Eight

Remember to Live!

Like an infant's open-eyed wonder
and the insights of a wise grandmother,
like a young man's vision for justice
and the vitality that shines in a girl's face,
like tears that flow in a friend bereaved
and laughter in a lover's eyes,
you have given me ways of seeing, O God,
you have endowed me with sight like your own.
Let these be alive in me this day,
Let these be alive in me.

—J. Philip Newell

One of the best-known stories told by Jesus in the Gospels is that of the Prodigal Son. It is usually invoked or reflected upon relative to the theme of forgiveness, but there is another way to read the story. The three characters—the father and his two sons—can be viewed as reflecting three different approaches to life.[1]

The elder son is a real straight shooter. He does not color outside the lines. His response to life is that it should be contained, controlled, and clear. He likes to know where things are at. He has a strong sense of duty and lives for his job. He wants to please and plays by the rules. He carries an active concern for his standing in the family. He appreciates the affection of others but does not seem very affectionate himself. When informed that his younger brother who was lost has returned home and that his father is throwing a party, his reaction is one of anger. There is disdain and resentment in his refusal to go in to the party. He would never make the mistakes of his brother. He would never allow himself to spend money frivolously or to fall prey to greed or lust. He is not like the rest of men, and sees himself as a cut above them. He will have nothing to do with those who sink to such depths. And it upsets him to see such behavior rewarded.

The younger son is filled with dreams of the world beyond his father's property. He is curious, adventuresome, ready to explore. Life is short and time is passing by, so he asks his father for his share of the estate, heads off for a foreign country, and proceeds to squander it on profligate living. Whatever he lives, he lives intensely, whether it's his flings with prostitutes or his hunger with the pigs. There is a restlessness in him. When he is with his family, he wants to roam. When he is on his own, he wants to come back. In every situation, the grass seems to be greener on the other side of the fence; whatever life is not his at the moment, that's what he wants. We see in him a response to life we normally associate with the young; we are willing to be patient with it as a phase, but when it does not end, it makes us sad. However, he can recognize a mistake when he's in front of it, and he's not above asking for forgiveness and making a fresh start.

The third approach is that of the father. Unlike his younger son, here is a man who enjoys the present, who knows how to live in the moment. Unlike his older son, he finds the positive side to things and does not allow himself to be filled with negativity when things are difficult. He has an irresponsible, immature son, and he loves him. He has an elitist, better-than-thou son, and he loves him, too. He loves them not because of what they do or don't do, but because he is their father.

We get the sense that the father is a lover of life. Unlike his older son who lacks spontaneity and passion, he has both in abundance. He runs down the road to meet his son and throws his arms around him. Whatever was on his agenda when his youngest appeared is now put aside and the word goes out: "We're having a party! Let there be music and dancing!" People and relationships come first.

This biblical story with its three different approaches to life asks: What's most important to us? What are the values that orient and motivate our living? The reflections in this chapter, while certainly of benefit to those in midlife as well, are offered particularly with those in their retirement years in mind.

The Important Questions

The book *Tuesdays with Morrie* is the true story of an elderly, dying college professor who spends his last Tuesdays on earth with a former student, Mitch Albom. Mitch relates a key moment in their conversations. He once asked Morrie—who was suffering from ALS, commonly known as Lou Gehrig's disease—whether, if it could be done, he would want someone to wave a magic wand and make him all better, make him the man he had been before.

> [Morrie] shook his head. "No way I could go back. I am a different self now. I'm different in my attitudes. I'm different about appreciating my body, which I didn't do fully before. I'm different in terms of trying to grapple with the big questions, the ultimate questions, the ones that won't go away.
>
> "That's the thing you see. Once you get your fingers on the important questions, you can't turn away from them."
>
> And which are the important questions?
>
> "As I see it, they have to do with love, responsibility, spirituality, awareness. And if I were healthy today, those would still be my issues. They should have been all along."[2]

Love

The field of possible reference is wide here, from erotic (passionate love, with sensual desire and longing), to familial (self-sacrificing, active, volitional, and thoughtful love), to platonic (chaste, loyal, affectionate love between friends). In different cultures and historic periods these have been variously named. C. S. Lewis, in his book *The Four Loves*, identifies four experiences—affection, friendship, Eros, charity—each with its own character and coloration.

Jesus put at the center of life's meaning that to love God with all your heart, mind, and strength, and to love your neighbor as yourself, are the two most important things in life (Mark 12:28–34). And his apostle John instructed us "to love one another, because love is from God....Whoever does not love does not know God, for God is love" (1 John 4:7–8). It is not by accident that the symbol of love is the human heart, because the heart of a fulfilled life is love. If we are going to remember to live, of this we must be a little more careful than of anything.

Family love and marital love and the affection among friends are hopefully familiar to us. The question is: To what extent are they intentionally cultivated realities, a source of joy and happiness for us, not in the abstract but in actuality, here and now?

We must make continual choices to keep love at the center. In my own work, one of the primary sources of joy, satisfaction, and fulfillment are weekend and weeklong retreats where people step back from their normal preoccupations, come together, and share from a deep place in their lives. These experiences, while at times physically draining, are rejuvenative on another level, and I emerge from them buoyed up in spirit, as though fed from a wellspring within.

Love in daily living wears many garments, depending on one's occupation, but the common experience that marks all its expressions is that of people being personal with one another. For a bus or cab driver, that means transforming the habitual routes by seeing not only traffic lights and street signs but the faces and conditions of the people who get on board and then by relating to them. For the doctor or nurse or dentist, it will mean seeing not a case or a chart or a cavity as much as a human being before them with particular needs and responding to them sensitively. For a retiree, it will mean seeing where help is needed within the home, the church, and civic communities.

When we serve the needs of others, we are acting in a God-like manner and we remain vibrant and motivated because there is nothing else as satisfying. Such is the renewing power of love, of desiring the good of another and doing whatever we are able to do to bring that good about.

We are all familiar with the Hollywood brand of romantic love on the big screen, but the kind that is closer to most of us looks more like care for aging parents or spouse or friends. It's not very glamorous; in fact, it can be downright messy. Writer Melissa Musick Nussbaum, for example, talks about caring for her mother who is eighty-nine, has macular degeneration, and is nearly deaf, but who will not wear her hearing aids; her mother who is unsteady on her feet and whose falls are becoming more frequent; her mother who talks—a lot—about her bowel movements, their color, consistency, and frequency.

It's not the picture Melissa had envisioned of her mother in her golden age, with her daughter sitting by her rocking chair, the two of them drinking tea and eating homemade cookies together, sharing abiding truths and wonderful stories of yesteryear. Melissa's fantasy was of heart-to-heart conversations in which her mother would reflect with her about facing aging and death gracefully with faith and dignity, and of how she would listen appreciatively and learn.

But the reality is that the phone rings at 7 a.m. and it's her mother, who has not slept well and whose knee hurts and who tells her by way of greeting that "I hate these damn childproof tops on my Tylenol bottles because I can't get them off!"

> It's not, I sometimes muse, Mitch Albom's *Tuesdays with Morrie*….Then I remember: Albom spent Tuesdays with Morrie. And not even Tuesday nights. Just Tuesdays. During the day. Working hours. I can stand anyone for one day a week during business hours. I want to read *24/7 with Morrie*….
>
> I'm not too interested in Tuesdays. I want to read about the daily-ness of old age, the daily-ness of sickness, the daily-ness of death, the daily-ness of care. I don't want to read about keepers. For, as any housekeeper knows, it is daily work, done better or worse, over and over again….
>
> I don't have to like it, or feel elevated by the work. I

just have to do it. And, task by task, I become a woman who brings order out of chaos. I become a woman who cleans what is dirty, who puts things right.

And as it is with the work of housekeeping, so I hope it is with the work of love. Just as sweeping is an act, and not a thought, so love is an act, and not a feeling. My work is to open the Tylenol bottle, to speak up and speak slowly, to offer my arm, to help her in and out of the car, to listen. Just that, song in my heart or not. And task by task, day by day, I become my mother's keeper.[3]

It is not without reason that this kind of love is at the core of the vows of newlyweds at the altar. It is what love looks like at its quintessential best: love as faithful, caring presence, "through good times and bad, in sickness and in health, till death do us part." And we never know when death will us part, so the actions of love—the choosing-to-love even when there's not a song in our hearts—are, yes, one of life's most important decisions. The fact is that relationships are life's blue-ribbon experience. They turn the dross of daily-ness into gold. They make human community real. They provide what we need and wait in turn for us to give back.

Michael, a lawyer, e-mailed his family the following message under the subject line "Don't Take It for Granted":

I spent Wednesday and Thursday of this week at the scene of an accidental death by electrocution. A longtime employee of one of our clients was killed when the bucket on the boom lift [cherry picker] he was operating somehow came in contact with a high-voltage power line overhead. The line was reportedly energized with 115,000 volts of electricity.

The man was forty-seven years old, with a wife and four children—ranging in age from eleven to sixteen. A picture of one of his daughters in her high school volleyball uniform was posted on the plywood wall immediately behind the driver's seat in his work van.

I am sure when he got up on Wednesday morning to go to work, it never occurred to him that he would not come home that evening. Those who knew him described him as "safe," "cautious," a "good man," a "family man." His brother showed up at the scene on Thursday morning and just sat and stared at the accident scene for over an hour. He could not believe this had happened to his brother, and he could not believe his brother was gone.

I know the subject line of this e-mail sounds rather trite. But the experience of the last few days has renewed for me the simple importance of the notion that life is fragile. This young man no longer has the opportunity to hug his wife and kids, or tell his family and friends how much they mean to him. Nor do they have an opportunity to tell him how much he meant to them.

We still do.

I hope you all have a great weekend. Take good care of and love each other. Engage in life to the fullest. I love you all.

In reminding his family to live life to the full, Michael put love at the center of the screen.

Responsibility

In 1992, 12 percent of the population of the United States was over sixty-five. By 2020, demographers tell us, 18 percent of the country will be over sixty-five.[4] Joan Chittister has observed in her book *The Gift of Years* that the season of life beyond sixty-five is not about diminishment, though there will inevitably be some of that. It is, instead, about giving ourselves over to a new kind of development. Our moral responsibility is to stay as well as we can, to remain active, to do the things that interest us, and to enrich the lives of those around us. Our spiritual responsibility is to age well and provide an inspiring example for others of the possibilities of this period of life. These years are for allowing the interior life to direct what we do and who we are, and to do so consciously, knowing that for all the losses, there are new things to gain as well. Now, perhaps for the first time, we have the freedom and the opportunity to decide what we really want to do with life rather than what we must do or should do. We have the chance to be the best self we have ever been, and to help others do the same. This is the time to do every single thing we can possibly do. There is nothing for which to save our energy. Now it is simply time to spend time well.[5]

In their fifties, Jackie and Dave knew something was wrong. Empty nesters, they realized their own relationship was at a low ebb. The smallest things started huge arguments. A communication course caught their attention. Without much enthusiasm they joined. One of the first questions posed was, "Think of a time when you were really happy together. What was going on?" Asked to write their answers and then share them, they were astounded that they had both written the same thing: "When we were volunteering overseas and exploring new countries together." They had started their married life in Japan in 1956 where Dave was a lab technician with the Air Force, and then, inspired by Tom Dooley, had given a year of service with the Presbyterian Mission Hospital and a new college in Taegu, Korea. Those had been interesting and enjoyable days.

After taking the communication course, Jackie and Dave ran across a book called *The Footpaths of Britain* by Michael Marriott, which introduced them to the idea of long-distance walking. They decided to give it a try. A two-week trek along the coast of Wales brought so much pleasure that it ushered in about a ten-year period when each vacation consisted of another walk in places like the Austrian Alps and Britain's Cornish coast. But then Dave's knee gave out. Walking became a downer. So he said, "Why not try biking?" Trail bike rides around the neighborhood were encouraging. Dave's knee was okay with biking. In their hiking days, they had learned about biking along the Danube River. Signing up with a company that rented bikes, made reservations, and carried their baggage, they biked from Passau in Germany to Budapest in Hungary. Along the way, riders told them of other rides along different rivers that were not too demanding, so another year, they explored the Altmühl River in Germany.

In their walking days, Jackie had given Dave the book *Walking Across Europe From Top to Bottom* by Susanna Margolis and Ginger Harmon. The idea of walking across Europe caught their imagination, but now was no longer possible. "What about biking it?" Dave wondered. This was intriguing. Dave pulled out maps and started plotting a route along river ways. In 2004, with both of them aged seventy, they cycled 2000 miles from Amsterdam to Marseilles over 126 days. This gave them such a high that they took five more long-distance trips in subsequent summers. Why do they keep going back? What do these experiences do for them? Jackie explains:

> You can't beat being outdoors every day, getting lots of exercise, seeing new places, and meeting new people. Having a destination is a great mental exercise. It pulls you forward. The day we rode into Helsinki, we were on a high. We were seventy and we'd just ridden across Scandinavia on bikes!
>
> We don't really train. The first few days we're sore and wobbly, but gradually we get stronger. There's lots of time to smell the flowers, talk with folks along the way, to sit on every bench we encounter and simply appreciate what's before us. Let's face it, we are getting older, so each trip has been a bit shorter with more rest days.

To help pay for their trips, Jackie and Dave have rented out their house during the summers. But as they age, getting the house ready for rental, packing the bikes for plane travel, and coming home to a garden full of weeds is more of a hassle. Also, they want to prepare for the time when living on their own is not possible. So they are joining a retirement community called Wake Robin near the shores of Lake Champlain south of Burlington, Vermont. Their bike trips have been good preparation for this new chapter of their lives.

> We'll be in a cottage with a third of the space we now have. When you live for a couple of months with two saddlebags of stuff, you realize that you can be happy with very little. Also we've learned that we thrive on newness—exploring new places, meeting new people. Moving to Vermont is a big adventure for us. Our son had advised us not to settle on just any place but to find somewhere that lights our fire. Wake Robin does. From our doorstep, we can bike to Montreal, Quebec, Buffalo, and New York City along routes that are flat and beautiful. Our first venture will be a circuit around Lake Champlain to explore our new home.

It would be a mistake to see Jackie and Dave's taking responsibility for their time and energy as a late-in-life development. When I first met Jackie and Dave in 1983, Dave was immersed in humanitarian assistance through his work in the Agency for International Development. Jackie was engaged with a group called the Partners Community, which she had helped cofound.

> Our mission at first was to demonstrate that Roman Catholics and Protestants could be partners in the faith. This was not the case when we started. Our partnership was so enriching that we wanted to make the treasures we were experiencing available to others. We all got trained in experiential faith development through the national organization Faith at Work, now renamed Lumunos, and also through the ecumenical Church of the Saviour. The method we used to share our message was the teaching of weekly classes. We would go out two by two, a Roman Catholic and a Protestant paired, and work in area churches. People found our courses life changing and wanted us to write them up so they could teach them. This we did.[6] When the books were published, the nature of our group changed. We diversified into individual missions and moved to a monthly meeting and an annual retreat, which is still our format even now. Each year we choose a theme and then develop it in the monthly gathering. As we grow older, our themes have related to aging, diminishment, and facing our mortality.

Jackie's sense of responsibility continues to open outward. Her latest work is *Our Defining Moment: A Pocket Guide to Creating the Future We Truly Want*. Available free online,[7] the book's aim is to help both individuals and organizations bring the world into a new renaissance. In the book she discusses four P's—planet, poverty, peace, and purpose—and offers key global and personal strategies to address each. As a grandmother, she wants to be sure her grandchildren and all grandchildren inherit a thriving world culture and a healthy planet:

> This juncture of history presents an extraordinary opportunity to create a positive future—a world that works for all.

The resources are out there to do so—the money, know-how, and people power. Each of us has a part to play that needs our particular talents and experience. The next step: say "yes" and add to the good things that are happening.

There are a lot of people out there who are looking for other people who will also take the time to do what really needs to be done—for the neighborhood, the city, the planet. They are looking for other people who also want to be involved with something not because it pays well, but because it's worth doing. If we're lonely, it may be because we have not looked around to see who needs us. And a person who is needed is never lonely, isolated, or without purpose in life.

At the heart of Jackie's vision is generativity—the act of giving ourselves to the needs of the rest of the world. It is the most important function in life's final quarter. A Harvard Medical School study on adult development indicated that the key factor in the achievement of successful aging is not money, not education, not family, but widening one's social circle, becoming actively involved in helping someone else.[8]

There is no such thing at any stage of human development as a fulfilling life without relationships. In this later stage then, the only question is whether we will decide to live inside ourselves—alone with our past relationships—or reach out in new encounters. This might be socially, in places where the generations mix and the fun comes from meeting new people and talking about different things, or in caretaking, supervising, coordinating, or volunteering.[9]

Here is a test to find whether your mission on earth is finished: If you're alive, it isn't. Remembering to live means accepting some responsibility and making a positive contribution to something, somewhere. The world is waiting with open arms.

Spirituality

Spirituality has to do with meaning or purpose in life; with heart-of-the-matter questions about what it means to be human, about who we are and why we are here. Every person has spiritual needs such as the need for relatedness and belonging, for hope and love and forgiveness. There are only two sources of love, acceptance, and forgiveness: people and God. We need both for happiness and fulfillment.

In our later years, we must look more deeply inside our own hearts and souls for the answers to our questions and problems. This is the season for becoming more honest with ourselves, for bringing unresolved questions or feelings of guilt from out of the shadows into the light where they can find a gentle, clarifying response or resolution.

This is the period for spiritual reflection and renewal, a time to ask ourselves what kind of person we have become. This time of life is not meant to simply freeze and confirm us in our inadequacies, but to free us for further growth. Have we become more or less compassionate, generous, and ready to listen and help through what we have lived? Can we develop or give more play to our sense of humor? Can we try our hand at something new? Can we speak our truth without needing the affirmation of others?[10]

These are the years where less stress allows us to open to the ecstasy of life and surrender to the Mystery called God. In our senior years, freed from the demands of work and stultifying routine, we can sit long in silent appreciation of a painting in an art gallery, a child playing in a sandbox, a flower opening its petals to the sun. We can experiment with a new recipe, sit in the recliner and listen to favorite music, schedule a massage in the middle of the day.

It is in these later years that our relationship with our Creator, the evaluation of our life goals and behaviors, and the consequent surrender to the spiritual meaning of life rather than simply to the material things of life come to the fore more than ever. For some it may seem like reactivating and finding new sense in things learned long ago—things that have been let go of to some degree but that never left completely. For others, it is a case of the questions becoming less about orthodoxy and more about the spiritual dimensions of life.

Spirituality becomes more important than ever for us as we begin to think about or enter into retirement because it is a positive way of seeing and living life. Our spiritual life is not a life beyond regular everyday existence; it can only be real if it is lived in the midst of the pains and joys of the here and now. It includes learning to live with an illness or serious challenge. It defies quantification and measurement, but it is clearly manifested in our character and behavior. Think of someone whose company you enjoy, someone whose naturalness, humor, transparency, and emotional availability all delight you and allow you to experience more of your own vitality than usual. Healthy spirituality always brings more life, draws forth good results in ordinary situations.

At thirty-eight, Mark Davis Pickup was forced by multiple sclerosis into taking medical retirement from a career in government. Like many of us, he had derived much of his identity from work. Now he is a writer and speaker about disability, life, and end-of-life issues. He says:

> I spent many years in the work world. There were places to go, people I needed to see, tasks that needed to be done—they could only be done by me. It was easy to delude myself that I was indispensable. Retirement told me it was all a lie and that I was not as indispensable as I had believed.
>
> Work carried on fine without me. The basket into which I had put the eggs of my exaggerated sense of self-importance had a false bottom that opened to send my delusions crashing at my feet.
>
> Retirement is an opportunity, not a sentence. It is a wonderful opportunity to redefine personal identity and priorities. It allows the retiree to start afresh and place faith, family, and community (in that order) front and centre in their lives. That's where they should have been all along.
>
> Work is a good and important thing, but not the most important thing. It should not be treated by our actions and priorities as though it were. We work to live, not live to work.
>
> When we keep this in mind, retirement will be easier because it can be seen as one of life's transitions.

Each transition is as important and vital to human development and internal growth as previous and future transitions. But most important, retirement is a marvelous time to draw closer to Christ and the people around us.

Retirement is not to be feared but embraced. As for this retiree, my new title is Christian, father, grandfather, and citizen. That's where my identity is now. It's the most important job I have ever had.[11]

Mark's spirituality enabled him to frame his trying circumstances in such a constructive way. Spirituality is a growing intimacy with God experienced through the people, places, events, and things of daily living. It is our response to life, everyday life, whose sacred essence shines through as we grow in the love of God and become more aware of and attentive to our neighbor's needs. It is expressed in everything we do, in what we support and affirm as well as in what we protest and deny.

Our spirituality is reflected in our behavior as we wait in line at the grocery store, in the way we drive our car, in how we use our leisure time, in who we befriend, and in where we decide to live. If we do not find God in everyday life, we risk missing God completely. Each of us has the two essentials for a rich spiritual life: our own personal experience, and the Holy Spirit present to us in it all.

Ultimately, no one can teach us how to bear adversity when we find ourselves alone and fearful. Care-givers and health-care workers can try to control the pain and nausea that patients experience, but they cannot provide peace of mind. That comes from within, from one's spirituality. Even suffering appears to belong to our transcendence, for it can take us beyond ourselves and put us in touch with our deepest selves. And if we believe there is a meaning in life, we will likely accept that there is also meaning even in suffering and death. "He who has a *why* to live can bear almost any *how*," as Friedrich Nietzsche is often alleged to have said.

As Mitch discovered with his friend Morrie, how we perceive a reality like death affects the way we live. How we live affects the way we die. And how we die gives new meaning to the way others can live.

Awareness

The tradition of Christian spirituality speaks about awareness and attention as an inner attitude of "stretching toward," as a focusing of the mind. Someone who is attentive is someone who reaches toward something. It's not so much the activity of a particular human faculty as much as a movement of the entire person, body and spirit. Once we have discovered the meaning, center, and goal of our existence, attention becomes the unification of our actions in the light of that goal, our profound dedication to that center. Thus, growing in awareness means growing in personal integration and unification.

This theme has come to the fore for many Christians in the interfaith encounter with Buddhists who speak about it in the language of "mindfulness." For Buddhists, it is through attention to whatever fills this moment that one reaches a penetrating vision of reality, a way of seeing beyond appearances and externals to an underlying unity of being.

Awareness relates to an attentiveness of the heart. The early Church father Basil of Caesarea, in commenting on the Bible verse "Be careful" (Deut 15:9), writes, "Pay attention to yourself if you want to pay attention to God." This attention to ourselves means being aware of and resisting the thoughts or impulses that draw us away from our center, that distract us with worldly seductions such as the modern addiction to pornography on the Internet. It becomes a way of guarding the heart and defending our inner life. Awareness in this sense is a discipline of the spiritual life and requires vigilance and constant struggle.[12]

Vigilance is the sobriety of those who have a clearly defined goal to pursue and who keep their eyes open, knowing that if they are not vigilant, they may be distracted from their goal. Basil, again: "What is it that defines the Christian? Keeping watch every day and hour and being ready to carry out what pleases God, in the knowledge that the Lord will come at an hour we do not expect." This kind of vigilance is the ability to think critically, with awareness of and involvement in the world in which we live, and freedom from dissipation. Such a person becomes *responsible*, aware of the need to pay attention to his or her surroundings, and in particular, capable of watching over others and taking care of them. Such watchfulness at the same time produces an inner equilibrium that creates unity between our faith and our life: we are asked not only to be watchful with regard to the world in which we live and those around us, but also with regard to ourselves, our own work, and our personal relationships. This kind of attentiveness allows God to reign in every aspect of our lives. However we might name it—awareness, attention, vigilance, watchfulness—it is the source of every virtue in the spiritual life, the salt that flavors all of our actions, and the light by which we think and speak.[13]

There is a Sufi story that describes how awareness like this transforms the water of each day's living into wine:

> Once upon a time a Sufi made the annual pilgrimage to Mecca. It was a long walk for him, and the sun was high. He had come miles without stopping. Finally, in the sight of the mosque at Mecca, sure of the goal now, the old man lay down in the road to rest.
>
> Suddenly, one of the other pilgrims shook him awake, rough and harsh in the doing of it. "Wake up," he commanded. "You blaspheme. You lie in such a way that your feet are pointed toward God in the holy mosque! What kind of Sufi are you?"
>
> The old Sufi opened one eye, smiled a bit, and said, "I thank you, holy sir. Now if you would be kind enough to turn my feet in some direction where they are not pointed toward God."[14]

Similarly, when our awareness detects the presence of God in the people and events of our day, it is no longer necessary to kneel to find God outside ourselves. Our souls are in a state of an eternal bow before the presence of God within us. The One to whom we reach out all our days reaches back to us in every time and place. The One who has been quietly at our sides all our lives becomes the object of our awareness and attention. The Other was always there, but we were not at home; now, there is no longer any distance or separation. There will of course be times when the Presence is less palpable, perhaps even times of darkness, but even then, there is a sense of companionship that never goes away. We have come to know and see and respond to life differently. We know now that we are no longer alone, and when we are confronted with the unknown, we immediately turn to the source of life within. For we know now that life is not ended but merely changed. So in this season, life plays in stereo for us, coming from two speakers simultaneously: from one side come the demands and possibilities of this earthly life, and from the other come inner sound waves of trust and strength, courage and guidance, to carry us far beyond the storms of the present to the fullness of the future. At this stage of our lives, we know that we are more than our public self. There is a soul-life within us that is clear and conscious.[15]

Passive and Active Aging

In her book *The Gift of Years*, Joan Chittister reflects on the two approaches to aging: passive and active. Passive aging sees the last season of life as a slow slide toward death. The natural changes of the body are accompanied by a creeping paralysis of the soul. Active aging works with the physical effects of age by adjusting the rhythm and pace. It does not see this season of life as a burden or a problem to be solved, but as a celebration to be lived. The person who is aging actively moves to a gentler form of exercise but stays active; offsets hearing loss by reading more; compensates for changes in eyesight by getting a good pair of headphones and listening to downloaded programs or CDs. Lifelong learning makes the difference between healthy and unhealthy aging, writes Chittister:

> It determines the degree to which life will be satisfying to us, as well as the degree to which we will be inter-esting, valuable, life-giving to others.

Ongoing learning saves the aging from becoming more fossilized than transformed. The problem with aging is not age; it is petrification, rigidity of soul, inflexibility. Only ideas keep ideas flowing. When we close our minds to what is new, simply because we decide not to bother with it, we close our minds to our responsibility to ourselves—and to others—to keep on growing.

Surely this capacity for ongoing learning and the sense of new meaning it brings to life is not an idle gift. Surely the very fact that it develops as we grow means that it is meant for something important. And when would that be more important than when life in all its physical dimensions becomes less accessible, less doable, less desirous? Why wouldn't this capacity for learning be exactly what is needed in a generation whose responsibility is to bring the wisdom of the years to the questions of the times?[16]

Fleurette Sweeney, a member of the Sisters of Charity of Halifax, Nova Scotia, has been involved in music education since she was thirty-eight. Folk-song games involving sensory/motor integration formed the basis for her master's thesis. She cofounded the Richard's Institute for Music Education and Research in California and for twenty years lived out of a suitcase teaching education through music across the United States. At sixty-two. she retired from the Institute and moved to British Columbia where she began teaching courses all over the province—but only with a master's degree. At sixty-seven, she began doctoral studies in the field of education and graduated at age seventy-three.

Before this, the last time I had worked in a library, it was with library cards. But now, it's a computer age. I started from scratch learning computer skills. It was fun working on my dissertation with these new instruments.

I learned so much about research. One course I took identified ten different forms of research, and we had to make samples from our own research and write them up in these different styles. It was thrilling to share research with people in so many different professions—forestry, medicine, literature, business, languages, science, you name it!

The title of my dissertation was "From Sound to Symbol." It was absolutely wonderful working on it! I'm presently doing all my work now under the auspices of the Living Language Institute Foundation in Vancouver. I'm now in my eighties and teaching programs for senior citizens and going about the province working with librarians. My favorite workshop in our highly immigrant city of Japanese, Mandarin, Tagalog, and Spanish speakers is "Creating a Language of Community." We use folk-song games as a way of evoking conversation between parents and children and grandparents. The languages of the earth are being lost. When you think of how a language forms a people, how it represents their wisdom about life...and now they're more and more limited to English. The global economy is colonizing their languages off the face of the earth. I've been an armchair student of economics and globalization, and it's taught me to look behind what's happening on the surface for its deeper meaning.

I've never considered this "work." It's been pure observation, intrigue, learning. I feel so blessed!

This is what remembering to live looks like in broad terms: staying engaged, seeing where there's a need and making a positive contribution, learning new things all along the way, and finding delight in the experience.

What Shall We Learn Now?

Needless to say, the question is not, Is the older generation still capable of learning? It is, rather, What shall we learn now? Shall we become even better at what we have always done? Become an expert in the field, a consultant in the region, an authority on the subject? Or shall we open new doors, like learning a language so as to help new immigrants in town; becoming a mentor for struggling students; leading cultural or historical tours in our local area; working with the local Meals-on-Wheels to deliver food to shut-ins?

A year after my father died, my mother at eighty-eight announced to me that she had rejoined the funeral choir at church. "My new ministry," she said, "is to visit the sick and bury the dead." When we go on giving ourselves away right to the very end, we have lived a full life. It would be so easy to allow ourselves to go to seed, to slowly dry up within. But retirement is not about whether we will work or not; it is about what our work will be and why we do it.

In the community in which I live, Jack, a former dean of canon law at Catholic University, now in his late eighties, oversees the community's central archives and responds to the questions that come by post or e-mail. And when I step to the window in the early morn, I generally see Bill, a maintenance engineer in his late seventies who wants to continue to render service, walking up the sidewalk to water the flowers and see that the electrical systems in the building are running as they should.

The invitation of our later years is to recognize their potential and know what to do with them. The opportunities are there to make new friends, travel to places we've never been, or take up a creative art like painting or knitting. Have we ever had a pet? Did we ever learn to fish? Did we ever try growing things in a garden?

And now that we're no longer in the authority role in the family, we can enjoy younger people more than we ever did before, welcoming them with an open door and open heart, judging them less, learning new things from them. We can call them instead of waiting for them to call or come for a visit. We can send them fun cards, take them to a play or to the zoo. We might even begin to think differently about some things as a result of our conversations with them!

Our senior years offer us the possibility of liberating ourselves from ourselves—from our routines, our workaholic compulsions, our constricted range of interests. The field of possibilities is as wide open as the doors to the local art gallery, library, or tour bus; as wide open as the entry to the park for bird-watching or the place next to the stranger on the bench ready to engage in the creative act of a conversation.

Are there people in our building or on the block who would appreciate someone picking something up for them—or someone with whom to play cards or go to a movie or simply talk? And what about those programs at our church we've never had time for before, like the prayer group or the Bible-study class or the food pantry or the choir or the new environmental group?

It's time to plan our days rather than simply let them slip by unnoticed.

What If You Had One Day...

We began this chapter with a conversation between Mitch and his former professor and friend, Morrie, about the important questions in life, but we stopped that conversation in midstream to reflect on those questions. Let's listen in again as that conversation—as well as the one we've been having here—ends. Mitch is trying to imagine Morrie as healthy again, as pulling the covers from his body, getting up from the chair, and going for a walk with him around the neighborhood, the way they used to walk around the campus. Suddenly, he realizes that it has been sixteen years since he'd seen Morrie standing up.

> What if you had one day perfectly healthy? I asked [him].
>
> "Let's see...I'd get up in the morning, do my exercises, have a lovely breakfast of sweet rolls and tea, go for a swim, then have my friends over for a nice lunch. I'd have them come one or two at a time so we could talk about their families, their issues, talk about how much we mean to each other.
>
> "Then I'd like to go for a walk, in a garden with some trees, watch their colors, watch the birds, take in the nature I haven't seen in so long now.
>
> "In the evening, we'd all go together to a restaurant with some great pasta, maybe some duck—I love duck—and then we'd dance the rest of the night. I'd dance with all the wonderful dance partners out there,

until I was exhausted. And then I'd go home and have a deep, wonderful sleep."

That's it?

"That's it."

It was so simple. So average. I was actually a little disappointed. I figured he'd fly to Italy or have lunch with the President or romp on the seashore or try every exotic thing he could think of. After all these months, lying there, unable to move a foot or a leg—how could he find perfection in such an average day?

Then I realized that was the whole point.[17]

Resources for Your Inner Work

Reflections

1. In the parable of the Prodigal Son, in which of the three approaches to life do you most see yourself represented—that of the younger son, the older son, or the father?
2. Write down the domains in which you presently exercise some responsibility, with a line or two describing your contribution in each area.
3. Identify a conference or two that interests you, as well as a few good books that would enlarge your view of the world or stretch your political vision.
4. Think of two or three people whose company you enjoy, people who exude a steadiness, an ongoing brightness. Look for an opportunity to talk with each one about the sources of their vitalizing energy.

Challenges

1. Make a list of the nonprofit organizations in your area that would welcome volunteer help. Is there one whose work interests you? Take the next step.
2. We have been made in the Creator's own image. At the very least, that means that each of us is endowed with some cre-

ativity. One of the best ways we can honor our Creator is to exercise our creativity. Is there a creative pursuit that you might enjoy investing some time and energy in, for example, gardening, cooking, painting, woodworking, music, knitting, writing, photography, or becoming more skilled on the computer? Decide on one and find out how to begin.

3. As discussed, awareness, attention, and vigilance relate to integrating and unifying the various aspects of our life toward the center and goal of our existence. How would you describe to another the goal of your existence? Is there an identifiable aspect of your own life (for example, work, sexuality, exercise, eating, relaxation, creativity) that is either a neglected or a wild child and that calls for greater awareness and integration? What concrete way can you address this?

Meditation

Read and reflect on the following passage by an anonymous writer:

I grew up in the forties and fifties with practical parents. A mother, God love her, who washed aluminum foil after she had cooked in it, then reused it. She was the original recycle queen, before they had a name for it. A father who was happier getting old shoes fixed than buying new ones.

Their marriage was good, their dreams focused. It was the time for fixing things. A curtain rod, the kitchen radio, the screen door, the oven door, the hem in a dress. Things we keep.

It was a way of life, and sometimes it made me crazy. All that refixing, eating, renewing. I wanted just once to be wasteful. Waste meant affluence. Throwing things away meant you knew there would always be more.

But then my mother died, and on that clear summer's night, in the warmth of the hospital room, I was struck with the pain of learning that sometimes there isn't any more.

Sometimes, what we care about most gets all used up and goes away, never to return. So, while we have it, it's best we love it, and care for it, and fix it when it's broken, and heal it when it's sick.

This is true for marriage, and old cars, and children with bad report cards, and dogs with bad hips, and aging parents and grandparents. We keep them because they are worth it, because we are worth it. Some things we keep. Like a best friend that moved away or a classmate we grew up with.

There are just some things that make life important, like people we know who are special, and so, we keep them close.

Question: Am I keeping them close?

How to Be Really Alive

Here are two different approaches to being really alive, one highlighting the place of leisure and fun, the other focusing on the fulfillment derived from responding to the needs of others.[18]

Ways to have more fun

Drink sunsets. Develop an astounding appetite for books. Stop worrying. Make "yes" your favorite word. Dry your clothes in the sun. Keep toys in the bathtub. Walk in the park with no destination. Play in the mud with a child. Invite your friends to a party just for the fun of it. Sing in the shower.

Five things God won't ask you on Judgment Day

1. God won't ask what kind of car you drove, but how many people you drove who didn't have transportation.
2. God won't ask the square footage of your house, but how many people you welcomed into your home.
3. God won't ask about the clothes you had in your closet, but how many you helped to clothe.
4. God won't ask how many friends you had, but to how many people you were a friend.
5. God won't ask in what neighborhood you lived, but how you treated your neighbors.

Exercise

1. Take a sheet of paper and write at the top of it, "How to Be Really Alive."

2. Create your own list or statement, combining something of the two approaches above, the fun and the frivolous with the serious.

3. Make sure that everything you write down is something you could realistically do within the next twelve months.

4. Post your sheet in a place where you will see it frequently.

Poem

A poem-response to Mitch Albom's question about Morrie: "How could he find perfection in such an average day? Then I realized that was the whole point!"

Circus Day

Today is going to be a circus day!
   Today you get to feel velvety water on human skin,
      listen to music standing smack between two speakers,
         squeeze the last drops from the grapefruit straight into
         your mouth
            warm your hands around a hot mug
              and experience how good it feels to pee.

And those are just the preliminary events!

In the skydome you can
   watch the chickadees dive and swoop but never crash,
      squint at sunbeams tap-dancing on sparkling water,
         applaud teams of ants pulling four times their weight,
            catch the illusions in sunlight and shadows,
              and witness clouds changing before your very eyes.

         And get this: there's no admission!
         You only have to show up—awake.

Prayer

I thank you, God
    for music
    and the warmth of the hearth,
    for walking trails in the woods
    covered with a carpet of autumn leaves.

I thank you for hot, homemade soup,
    bread fresh from the oven,
    and the cold, refreshing water of running streams;
    for the gratuity of the stars at night
    and the sky's color at dawn and dusk.

I thank you for the smile that melts the cold heart,
    the laughter that dissolves tension,
    the comfort of a friend's presence,
    for our bodies that tremble and
    surge with energy at a gentle caress.

I thank you for so many years of life,
    so many people met,
    so many lives shared,
    so many telephone calls and emails,
    so many soft snowfalls and summer evenings.

I thank you, God.
    If the curtain fell now,
    it would fall on a player in full bow,
    grateful for the part entrusted to him
    and for the message he was given to speak.

Appendix

Peace through Planning

Planning your funeral, like writing your obituary, is a sobering task. But those who do it leave a precious gift to their family members who, in a time of grief, sometimes are unable to think clearly. They will be grateful for every indication of your preferences. This helpful resource, "Peace through Planning," is graciously made available here by its author, Sr. Pauline Fritz, SSND. In it you will find a list of the general information that any adult, but particularly the elderly or dying, should have at hand. You will also find an explanation of the Catholic funeral rite and a convenient format in which to record important end-of-life decisions related to funeral planning (list of songs and scripture readings), roles family members and friends might be asked to play, as well as the rite of committal at the gravesite. Members of other churches are invited to use and adapt whatever elements presented here coincide with the funeral rites in their own traditions.

Here are the key elements of the planning resources covered in this guide:

    I. The Gathering of General Data
   II. Funeral Arrangements
  III. Overview of the Funeral Rite
  IV. The Funeral Mass
   V. The Rite of Committal at the Gravesite
  VI. Suggested Songs for the Funeral Liturgy
 VII. Suggested Readings for the Liturgy of the Word

I. The Gathering of General Data

Death comes to each of us. Often we have very little forewarning or control over the circumstances of our dying. Sudden death or death following a terminal illness remains part of the mystery of life. Planning for the end of our earthly life is a gentle way of being supportive of our loved ones who, while grieving our dying, must also try to make a peaceful, orderly, and spiritual transition to living without us. This guide is designed to make planning for our death a logical step in the life of a responsible and caring adult. After filling in the appropriate sections, place the guide in a safe but readily accessible location, along with one's health care directives, will, military discharge forms, insurance policies, insurance information, and other important documents.

Note: Immediate access to documents in a safe-deposit box may be legally restricted directly upon the person's death; therefore, these documents may not be readily available for health care or funeral planning and for other expenses. A different location is recommended.

Valuable Documents and Their Location

There is no time in adulthood when good health and safety are not dependent on the good will and reasonable activity of those around us. We live in hope. We depend on a loving Providence. Because we live with a margin of the unknown, we take prudent steps to plan for what we cannot control. First among these steps is the preparation of a Health Care Directive.

Health Care Directive

A health care directive is a written statement that enables you to inform others of the kinds of health care you would or would not want. By stating your preferences, you are assisting loved ones, doctors, and other health care providers to make medical decisions about your care if you are unable to do so yourself.

In order for a health care directive to be effective:

- It must be a written document.

- It must be signed and dated in the presence of two witnesses or a notary public.
- It must then be signed by the two witnesses or the notary public to verify it.

Neither of the witnesses may be heirs to the estate. Only one witness may be a health care provider providing direct care to the directive's writer.

After you have prepared a health care directive, copies should be made for:

- your doctor
- your health care provider
- your hospital
- your close family members

Laws governing health care directives are not the same in every state. Also, directives written in one state may not be enforceable in another state if the directives are not consistent with the laws of that state. Persons who live in other than their home state for extended periods of time should check the laws in that state.

A health care directive is not the same thing as a last will and testament. Unlike a last will and testament, which is enforceable through the probate court system, a health care directive must be followed to the extent allowed by reasonable medical practice. It is important to prepare a health care directive because you have the right to name the kind of health care you desire.

Health care directives do not and cannot be construed to condone, authorize, or approve mercy killing, euthanasia, suicide, or assisted suicide.

Power of Attorney

Power of attorney is a legal document in which you give another person the authority to make decisions regarding your financial, business, and legal affairs. It does not cover decisions about health care in most states. The document must contain the date it was signed and be witnessed by two adults or by a notary public. You may revoke the power of attorney at any time by canceling or destroying the document or may verbally or in writing express the intent to do so.

Your Personal Will

A will tells everyone how to divide the property and other holdings you have accumulated over your lifetime.

It is important to plan for the disposition of personal property. If a person dies without a will, state statutes will decide how to divide property among possible heirs. If no heirs can be found, the property may go to the state, instead of to persons or charities that were the intended beneficiaries. If your last will and testament cannot be located, it has the same effect as if no will had ever been prepared.

A will may contain a codicil (an attached document adding something to the will) that gives explicit instructions for giving away special things of limited monetary value to special people. It is important to remember that the will provides directions for the distribution of the assets of your estate. Your estate is the property you own as well as the debts you owe at the time of your death. Life insurance or other insurance policies that list a specific beneficiary will be paid to the specific beneficiary, and are in most cases excluded from the estate.

When preparing a last will and testament, give some thought to the needs of those for whom you wish to provide financial support after your death. You may choose to provide an inheritance or gifts for children, grandchildren, or other relatives. You may decide that you want some of your estate to be given to the Church or a favorite charity. The most important thing to remember is that these choices are your choices. If you die without a last will and testament, these choices will be made for you by others in accordance with applicable law.

In most cases, a last will and testament is prepared by an attorney. A last will and testament does not need to be prepared by an attorney to be valid. However, an attorney may be able to assist you in preparing your last will and testament in a manner that ensures that it complies with your wishes and is enforceable.

Saving the Data

Some people choose to keep a copy of their will with their health care directive and to give another copy to the person given power of attorney. The existence and location of this data should be shared with loved ones.

II. Funeral Arrangements

The following paragraph is intended to free the survivors from undue constraint in planning the funeral of the undersigned:

I have given the following instructions as an aid to my family and friends in the event of my death. I understand that some of these instructions may not be able to be carried out. Ultimately, my funeral should be an experience that helps my family and friends deal with the reality of my death. I understand and expect that the instructions I have given here may need to be changed because of the circumstances and/or the needs of my family and friends. These instructions are intended to be a guide, not an obstacle to a meaningful funeral.

_____

Name

_____

Signature

_____

Date

If you have not preplanned your funeral, but have given someone power of attorney, such decisions as funeral arrangements, all financial matters, and the execution of one's will become the responsibility of that person. It may be helpful to inform your power of attorney or family (if no power of attorney has been named) about the following areas:

People to Help Make Funeral Arrangements

The person(s) who could best help make my funeral arrangements are:

_____

Name

_____

Address

_____

Phone

Name

Address

Phone

Name

Address

Phone

People to Help Handle Financial Arrangements

The person(s) who could best help with my business and legal affairs are:

Name

Address

Phone

Name

Address

Phone

Name

Address

Phone

The time of your death may be very stressful for those who must be attentive to the details surrounding the funeral, the liturgy, and the burial. Loved ones may be expected to notify family and friends, select a casket and a cemetery plot, and plan for the visitation. Family and friends may also be invited to help plan the funeral liturgy, along with the pastoral staff of the church where the funeral will be held, so that the community can be led in prayer and worship services that reflect the life of and honor the memory of the deceased. Planning the funeral liturgy is an important part of the final farewell.

For persons who have time to anticipate the end of their lives, this section will provide guidance as you record information that will assist family and friends during funeral planning. You may complete this section by yourself, with family and friends, or with the help of the parish pastoral staff. The parish staff wants to make the planning of this farewell prayer a meaningful experience for those who gather to pray and remember.

Planning Suggestions

- Include all concerned persons in the funeral/liturgy planning.
- Use this guide in selecting prayers, songs, and scripture readings. Use a Bible or parish songbook when planning the liturgy.
- Ask parish staff to assist you in locating these books.
- Speak with the parish director of music about hymn selections.
- Ask the parish secretary to assist you in contacting the appropriate parish ministers who will help if you want a luncheon served after the liturgy.

Funeral Home

Arrangements with a funeral home of your choice, if not made before your death, should be begun by the family soon after your death. The complete services of the funeral home will then be available to them. The funeral home of your choice should be named here:

_____

Name

_____

Address

_____

Phone

The Viewing

Viewing the body is an important part of the grieving process. Most people prefer an open casket. If the funeral home recommends a closed casket, or if the family prefers a closed casket, it still may be beneficial to have a private viewing for the immediate survivors and/or very close friends. This can be arranged with the director of the mortuary.

Embalming

Embalming is necessary if viewing is desired or if funeral rites will occur more than seventy-two hours after the death. If cremation is chosen and the body is presented for viewing, then embalming is still required.

Clothing for the Deceased

The deceased will need a complete set of clothing, including undergarments. Shoes are optional. Jewelry may be placed on the deceased for the viewing and removed before the funeral service, if the family wishes. A rosary and crucifix may be placed in the casket if desired. If you have a preference for certain clothes or for certain jewelry to wear during the viewing, list them here:

_____

_____

Casket Bearers

There are usually six casket bearers (male or female) who assist in moving the casket at the church and cemetery. Usually family members or friends of the deceased are asked to serve as casket bearers. Serving as a casket bearer is an honor.

Sometimes honorary casket bearers are named. These people do not assist in carrying the casket but are named because of a special friendship or relationship with the deceased. Any number of individuals may serve as honorary casket bearers.

If you would like to ask particular people to be a main or honorary casket bearer, please name them here:

_____

_____

_____

_____

_____

Burial or Cremation as Final Disposition

Burial symbolizes the return of the body to the basic earthly elements from which it was made and from which it will be called to resurrection. The cemetery plot provides a location for the survivors to honor the deceased. While many people prefer burial of the remains as they remember the deceased, others have expressed a desire to be cremated. Cremation has been permissible in the Catholic Church since 1963, although burial of the body is clearly preferred. In the case of cremation, it is preferable that the body be present for the funeral Mass with cremation to follow, as the presence of the deceased's body more clearly evokes the Church's conviction that the human body is in Christ a temple of the Holy Spirit and is destined for future glory at the resurrection of the dead. After cremation, a private service of burial is arranged with the family. The cremated remains, or cremains, are placed in consecrated ground or a proper place of respect such as a mausoleum or a columbarium, which only holds funerary urns.

Please indicate how you want your body to be handled:

_____ I would like my body to be buried in a casket in a cemetery.

_____ I would like the cremated remains of my body to be placed in a worthy vessel and to be buried in a grave or entombed in a mausoleum or columbarium.

Memorials

In faith we pray for those who have died. Some memorial donations are left with a request to remember the deceased at Mass. Other people prefer memorial donations go to favorite charities as an appropriate way to be remembered.

Please show your own preference here:

_____ I appreciate being remembered in memorial Masses.
_____ I would like memorial donations given to:

_____
Organization

_____
Address

_____
Organization

_____
Address

III. Overview of the Funeral Rite

The death and resurrection of Jesus gives new meaning to the death of a Christian. For us, life is changed, not ended. We believe that in prayer we have a powerful way of being with our loved ones who have passed from death to life.

The funeral rite consists of the prayer vigil or wake, the funeral Mass, and the burial. During the funeral rite, the family and friends of the deceased share with the greater community their sense of loss. In turn, the community provides hope and comfort through the shared prayers of the funeral liturgy.

The Vigil or Wake Service

The wake service can be held either at the funeral home or in the church. Because friends and relatives come with memories to share and stories to tell, the wake service has a personal dimension.

A brief prayer service is part of the wake service. Similar to the Liturgy of the Word at Mass, the prayer service includes a greeting, a prayer for the living and the dead, a psalm, a reading from the scriptures, a few reflections by the prayer leader, and some intercessions.

A tribute may be part of the wake service. During this less-structured aspect of the wake service, family and friends are invited to share personal memories about the deceased. The individual tributes speak of the impact that the dead person had on the lives of others and the community.

The wake service is prepared by the family with help as requested from the parish staff.

In addition to or instead of tributes, the wake service may include a favorite poem or songs or hymns that may not be appropriate for the eucharistic liturgy.

Memory Table

A memory table is another way of remembering the deceased. The memory table may contain photographs, mementos of special occasions, items symbolic of one's work or hobbies, insignia of office or organizational membership, or other items that are representative of the life of the deceased.

Number of Services

At times, if the deceased belonged to a group or groups that hold their own prayer service, for example, the Knights of Columbus, Council of Catholic Women, or Veterans of Foreign Wars, the family is asked to make a decision about the number of services they wish. For some, the parish service alone is ideal. Specific groups could be incorporated into the parish service as an honor guard during the actual prayer. Others may choose to have a separate wake service to accommodate a specific group. More than two services are usually too tiring, even though visitation does bring support to the bereaved.

IV. The Funeral Mass

The funeral Mass is the second part of the funeral rite and is important in celebrating the life of the deceased as a member of the Christian community. Therefore, it is important that the funeral Mass is public, not private, so that the whole community can share emotional and spiritual support with the living. This guide, if completed by the deceased and/or family members, may be helpful in planning with the liturgist and presider of the funeral Mass.

Entrance Procession

Bringing the casket to the church and moving the casket to the altar symbolize the journey of the deceased from life into life eternal. Songs for this sacred event should be appropriate to a funeral liturgy.

The presider and assistants meet the casket and mourners near the church door. After greeting the mourners, the priest sprinkles the casket with holy water in remembrance of the person's baptism. A white cloth (pall) is placed on the casket by family members or friends in remembrance of the white garment received at baptism. A religious symbol such as a crucifix or Bible may be placed on the casket by a family member or friend. The presider then turns and leads the procession to the front of the church. This action is accompanied by an opening psalm or song.

The Easter Candle, placed near the coffin, is a reminder of the promise of Jesus to raise us up on the last day.

Placing of the Pall (White Cloth on Casket)

The pall is to be placed by

Placing of Religious Symbol on the Pall (Optional)

The symbol chosen

The symbol is to be placed by

Name of the Procession Song

Liturgy of the Word

The Liturgy of the Word consists of a reading from the Old Testament, a psalm or song, a reading from the New Testament (other than the gospels), and a gospel reading. Since the gospel is the retelling of Jesus' life, death, and resurrection, it stands at the center of Christian belief and as the centerpiece of the scripture readings at all liturgies. Because of the central position of the gospel in the Mass, those planning a funeral service should select the gospel passage first. The person who delivers the homily will look to the gospel passage you have selected for guidance in planning the homily.

In reading through the possible Old and New Testament selections, you may also find one that you would like to have read at the funeral home or the cemetery. Be sure to note it down.

The first two readings and the psalm (if it is not sung) may be read by a person or persons of your choice. Before asking a family member or friend to read a scripture passage during the funeral Mass, consider whether they will be willing to read in such a public setting. The priest or deacon will read the gospel and give a brief homily based on the paschal mystery of the Lord as proclaimed in the readings. Following the prayer after communion, a member or friend of the family may speak in remembrance of the deceased. The eulogy may also be given during the wake service.

Old Testament Reading

Passage chosen; list book, chapter, and verse

Read by

Responsorial Psalm

Passage chosen; list book, chapter, and verse

Read by

New Testament Reading

_____

Passage chosen; list book, chapter, and verse

_____

Read by

Gospel Passage

_____

Passage chosen; list book, chapter, and verse

_____

Read by

Homilist

_____

General Intercessions

General intercessions are read after the homily. These intercessions may be selected by you from those already in the funeral ritual, or they may be composed by family members and friends. The intercessions are read by a person of your choice immediately after the homily. If you choose to write your own intercessory prayers, those included below may serve as possible choices or as helpful models.

Persons leading the intercessory prayers begin by inviting the community gathered to respond to each petition with "Lord, hear our prayer." (See below.)

Leader: Please respond to each intercession with *Lord, hear our prayer.*

1. God of life, death, and resurrection, we believe that
   _____ lives on in eternal glory because of Jesus.
   Strengthen that faith in us who mourn. We pray to the
   Lord: *Lord, hear our prayer.*
2. For the family and friends gathered here, that God will
   comfort them in the knowledge that they will someday

be united with _____ in the loving presence of our
God. We pray to the Lord: *Lord, hear our prayer.*

3. Like you, Lord, _____ walked the path of suffering.
We thank you for the example of patience and courage
that characterized his/her life. We pray for courage and
faith to accept our pain of loss. We pray to the Lord:
Lord, hear our prayer.

4. That the family of _____ and all those who loved
him/her will find comfort in remembering the good
times and the love they shared. We pray to the Lord:
Lord, hear our prayer.

5. For God's blessings on all who lovingly supported and
cared for _____ in his/her last illness. We pray to
the Lord: *Lord, hear our prayer.*

6. Like you, Lord, _____ lived only a short time. [Use
this only when appropriate.] We thank you for his/her
love and friendship. We pray for courage and faith in
accepting our pain of loss. We pray to the Lord: *Lord,
hear our prayer.*

7. For the friends and members of our families who have
gone before us and await the kingdom. Grant them an
everlasting home with your Son. We pray to the Lord:
Lord, hear our prayer.

8. For _____, who in baptism was given the pledge of
eternal life, that he/she may now enjoy the company of
the saints. We pray to the Lord: *Lord, hear our prayer.*

Other Intentions for the Prayers of the Faithful

_____

_____

_____

Liturgy of the Eucharist

Preparation of the Gifts

The gifts of bread and wine are presented by two or more persons you have designated, while an appropriate hymn is usually sung. The altar and the gifts of bread and wine may be incensed at this time.

Bread and wine to be presented by

Name of hymn

Communion

During the Eucharistic Prayer the acclamations are sung. The acclamations are followed by the Lord's Prayer and the Sign of Peace. The congregation hopes and believes that our deceased loved one shares in God's eternal peace and so we extend that same peace to one another during the Sign of Peace. Family members or friends who already serve as eucharistic ministers may serve that role here. A hymn is sung during the distribution of the Eucharist.

Names of eucharistic ministers

Name of communion hymn

Words of remembrance to be spoken by

Name of the song of farewell

Closing

The Mass closes as usual with prayer. Also, the casket is incensed at this time as a sign of the great reverence we have for the body, which during life was the "temple of God." This incensing also symbolizes the rising of the person as well as our prayers into God's presence.

Name of recessional hymn

V. The Rite of Committal at the Gravesite

The third and final part of the funeral, the rite of committal at the gravesite, may be more private and is often the most painful aspect of the funeral rite. Death and burial have incredible finality. Generally, only those closest to you and the family will journey this last distance with you. Sometimes the committal at the gravesite takes place immediately after the funeral liturgy. Others choose to have the gravesite service after they have shared a meal with the family and friends who joined in the funeral Mass. Persons who choose cremation may have a private burial at a later date.

A funeral at a national cemetery may include an honor guard and an appropriate brief military ceremony. The funeral director will be able to provide you with information as to what is usual and customary under the circumstances.

The gravesite service consists of a blessing of the site (if this has not already been done), a scripture reading, intercessions, the Lord's Prayer, and the commitment of the body to the ground. The focus of the gravesite service is the commitment of the body to the earth from which it came. The lowering of the body symbolizes a final release of the body to its Creator.

The sacred place of burial is identified by a marker as requested by the deceased or planned by those who remain.

For those who have experienced the loss of a loved one, the celebration of that life may bring some closure; but for those who remain, *life is also forever changed.*

VI. Suggested Songs for the Funeral Liturgy

"Amazing Grace"
"Ave Maria"
"Behold the Lamb"
"Be Not Afraid"
"Here I Am, Lord"
"How Great Thou Art"
"I Am the Bread of Life"
"I Have Loved You"
"On Eagle's Wings"
"Our Father"
"Praise to the Lord"
"Shepherd me, O God"
"Shelter Me, O God"
"Song of Farewell"
"Stay with Me"
"The Lord Is My Shepherd"
"We Shall Rise Again"
"We Walk by Faith"
"You Are Mine"

VII. Suggested Readings for the Liturgy of the Word

For each passage below, its location in the Bible is given by the book's name, followed by the chapter and verse. Numbers in parentheses refer to the Lectionary for Mass as well, which is available from the parish. A summary of each passage below is also given in parentheses.

Old Testament

Job 19:1, 23–27a (Job's prayer of confidence in God)

Proverbs 31:10–13, 19–20, 30–31 (A worthy wife is to be praised)

Ecclesiastes 3:1–11 (#453) (To everything there is a season)

Wisdom 3:1–9 *or* 3:1–6 (Death is not the end, but the hope of immortality)

Wisdom 4:7–15 (Confidence that one who dies young has lived a full life and is with God)

Sirach 44:1, 10–15 (I will praise our ancestors)

Isaiah 25:6a, 7–9 (The promise of the kingdom's conquest over grief)

Isaiah 35:1–6, 10 (#7) (Now will the eyes of the blind be opened)

Isaiah 41:8–10, 13 (#821:3) (Peace! Peace to the far and near)

Isaiah 61:1–3 (#719:6) (God has sent me to comfort all who mourn)

Isaiah 65:17–21 (#245) (No longer will there be weeping and mourning)

Ezekiel 34:11–16 (I will watch over my sheep)

Ezekiel 37:12–14 (#34) (I will open your graves, my people)

Lamentations 3:17–26 (Grief gives way to hope)

Daniel 12:1–3 (At the second coming, the faithful will rise)

Micah 6:6–8 (#737:17) (Do right, love goodness, walk humbly)

Zephaniah 3:16–20 (#811:4) (I will gather you up and
bring you home)
2 Maccabees 12:43–46 (It is good to offer prayers for the
dead)

Responsorial Psalms

Psalm 23:1–3a, 3b–4, 5, 6 (The Lord is my shepherd;
there is nothing I shall want)
Psalm 25:6–7bc, 17–18, 20–21 (To you, O Lord, I lift up
my soul)
Psalm 27:1, 3, 7, 8b, 9a, 13, 14 (The Lord is my light and
my salvation)
Psalm 42:2, 3, 5 (My soul is thirsting for the living God;
when shall I see God face to face?)
Psalm 43:3, 4, 5 (Put your hope in God)
Psalm 63:2–3a, 3bc–4, 5–6, 8–9 (My soul is thirsting for
you, O Lord)
Psalm 103:8–10, 13–14, 15–16, 17–18 (The Lord is kind
and merciful)
Psalm 115:5, 6; Psalm 116:10–11, 15–16ac (I will walk in
the presence of the Lord)
Psalm 122:1–2, 3–4a, 4b–5, 6–7, 8–9 (I rejoiced when I
heard them say: let us go to the house of the Lord)
Psalm 130:1–2, 3–4ab, 4c–6, 7–8 (Out of the depths I cry
to you, Lord)
Psalm 143:1–2, 5–6, 7ab–8ab, 10 (O Lord, hear my
prayer)

New Testament

Acts 10:34–43 *or* 10:34–36, 42–43 (Jesus Christ is forgive-
ness for those who believe)
Romans 5:5–11 (Jesus' death—a testimony of God's love)
Romans 5:17–21 (The grace of Jesus overcomes our
offenses)
Romans 8:14–23 (Children of God; we are heirs with
Christ)

Romans 8:31b–35, 37–39 (Nothing can come between us
   and the love of Christ)
Romans 14:7–9, 10b–12 (Alive or dead, we belong to the
   Lord)
1 Corinthians 15:20–24a, 25–28, or 20–23 (All will be
   brought to life in Christ)
1 Corinthians 15:51–57 (Death is conquered by Jesus
   Christ)
2 Corinthians 5:1, 6–10 (We have an everlasting home
   with Christ)
Ephesians 3:14–21 (#476) (Experience a love beyond
   telling)
Philippians 3:20–21 (Our bodies will be glorified)
1 Thessalonians 4:13–18 (The glory of the resurrection)
2 Timothy 2:8–13 (If we have died with him, we shall live
   with him)
2 Timothy 4:6–8, 17–18 (#591) (I have finished the race)
1 Peter 1:3–9 (#44) (We are given a new birth)
Revelation 14:13 (Happy are those who die in the Lord)
Revelation 20:11—21:1 (The dead have been judged
   according to their works)
Revelation 21:1, 5a, 6b–7 ("I am the Alpha and the
   Omega")
Revelation 22:1–7 (#508) (We shall see God face to face)

Gospel Readings

Matthew 5:1–12a (The Beatitudes)
Matthew 6:19–23 (#369) (Where your treasure is, there
   your heart is)
Matthew 11:25–30 ("Come to me, all you who are
   weary")
Matthew 25:1–13 (Parable of the bridesmaids; the
   suddenness of death)
Matthew 25:31–46 (Parable of the last judgment)
Mark 15:33–39; 16:1–6 (Jesus gave out a cry and breathed
   his last)

Luke 1:67–74 (#201) (You shine on those who sit in the shadow of death)

Luke 7:11–17 (The raising of the widow of Nain's son)

Luke 12:35–40 (Waiting for the arrival of the master)

Luke 23:33, 39–43 ("Today you will be with me in paradise")

Luke 23:44–49; 24:1–6a ("Into your hands I commend my spirit")

Luke 24:13–35 (The appearance of Jesus on the road to Emmaus)

John 3:13–17 (#638) (All who believe will have eternal life)

John 5:37–40 (Whoever believes in Jesus has eternal life)

John 6:51–59 ("If anyone eats this bread, they will live forever")

John 10:11–18 ("I am the good shepherd")

John 10:27–30 ("I give my sheep eternal life")

John 11:17–27 ("I am the Resurrection and the Life")

John 11:32–45 (The raising of Lazarus)

John 12:23–38 (If a grain of wheat falls on the ground…)

John 14:1–6 (There are many rooms in the Father's house)

John 17:24–26 ("Father, all those you gave me I would have in my company")

Notes

Introduction

1. Maurice Gardiol, Josette Morel, Cosette Odier, and Thomas Ryan, *Souviens-toi de Vivre!* (Le Mont-sur-Lausanne, Switzerland: Editions Ouverture, 2007).

2. For more information on such retreats and congregational renewal events (titled Gospel Call), see http://www.paulist.org/unity/gospel_call.php.

1. Aging

Opening quotation is from Joan Chittister, *The Gift of Years* (New York: BlueBridge, 2008), 131.

1. Jonathan Trudel, "Vivre sans Vieillir," *l'Actualité*, July 2008, 22–31.

2. Eknath Easwaren, "The Quest for Immortality," *Blue Mountain: A Journal for Spiritual Living* 11:2 (Spring 2000): 1, 5, 6.

3. Leo Lefebure, *The Buddha and the Christ* (Maryknoll, NY: Orbis, 1993), 7–11.

4. Sir Lawrence Brotherton, http://s-g-m.net/readers.htm (accessed 1997).

5. Chittister, *The Gift of Years*, 24.

6. Joan Raymond, "How to Talk about Aging," *Newsweek* (June 18, 2007), 59.

7. Chittister, *The Gift of Years*, 14.

2. Illness

Opening quotation is from Enzo Bianchi, *Words of Spirituality* (Glasgow: Omnia Books, 2002), 106.

1. Henri J. M. Nouwen, "Out of Love, Into Love," *Pray* (March–April 1994), 6.

2. Kathryn Spink, *The Miracle, The Message, The Story: Jean Vanier and L'Arche* (Toronto: Novalis, 2005), 177.

3. Ibid., 224.

4. Bianchi, *Words of Spirituality*, 107–8.

5. This talk by Dr. Elisabeth Kübler Ross, MD, was originally given at a conference of the Association for Holistic Health in 1976. It also appeared in *Co-Evolution Quarterly* 14 (Summer 1977).

6. Edward Stevens, *Spiritual Technologies* (New York/Mahwah, NJ: Paulist Press, 1990), 89–93, slightly adapted. Used with permission.

7. Adapted from a reflection proposed by Anthony de Mello, SJ, *Hearts on Fire* (St. Louis, MO: The Institute of Jesuit Resources, 1993), 18–19.

3. Practicing the Little Letting Go's

1. Peter C. Phan, *Responses to 101 Questions on Death and Eternal Life* (New York/Mahwah, NJ: Paulist Press, 1997), 55.

2. Eucharistic Prayer II from the English translation of *The Roman Sacramentary* © 1985, International Committee on English in the Liturgy, Inc. All rights reserved.

3. Richard Rohr, *Beginner's Mind*, CD (Albuquerque, NM: Mustard Seed, 2002).

4. William Sloane Coffin Jr., as quoted in Thomas Ryan, *Wellness, Spirituality, and Sports* (New York/Mahwah, NJ: Paulist Press, 1986), 33–34.

5. Laurence Freeman, "Meditation and Dying," talk delivered at the International Congress on Palliative Care held in Montreal, October 1988.

4. The Good Death

Opening quotation is from Dr. Nuala Kenny, "Palliative Care in Line with Catholic Tradition," *Prairie Messenger* (December 1, 2010), 1.

1. John Donne, Meditation XVII from *Devotions Upon Emergent Occasions*, in *John Donne: The Major Works*, ed. John Carey (New York: Oxford University Press, 1990, 2008), 344.

2. Elisabeth Kübler-Ross, *Death and Dying* (New York: Macmillan Publishing Inc., 1969).

3. Raniero Cantalamessa, OFM Cap, "God Created Man for Life, Not Death," Gospel Commentary for the Feast of All Souls' Day (Rome, November 2, 2007), http://www.zenit.org/article-20893?l= English.

4. Matthew Philips, "Beliefwatch: Reincarnate," *Newsweek* (August 27, 2007), 14.

5. Robin Marantz Henig, "Will We Ever Arrive at the Good Death?" *New York Times Magazine* (August 7, 2005), 26–35, 40, 68.

6. As quoted in ibid., 35.

7. Libby Purves, "Something in the Way He Died," *The Tablet* (December 2001), 1734.

8. John O'Donohue, *Death: The Horizon Is in the Well*, tape six in the 8-CD series *Anam Cara: Wisdom from the Celtic World* (Louisville, CO: Sounds True, 1996).

9. Kenneth L. Woodward and John McCormick, "The Art of Dying Well," *Newsweek* (November 25, 1996), 61–67.

10. Ibid., 63.

11. Cardinal Joseph Bernardin, *The Gift of Peace* (Chicago: Loyola Press, 1996), 59, 71.

12. Benedict J. Groeschel, CFR, *Arise from Darkness: What to Do When Life Doesn't Make Any Sense* (San Francisco: Ignatius Press, 1995), 147, 148.

13. Dr. Ira Byock, *Dying Well* (New York: Putnam/Riverhead, 1997).

14. Ronald Rolheiser, "Life's Key Question" (October 9, 2005), http://www.ronrolheiser.com/columnarchive/?id=88.

15. Henri J. Nouwen, *Life of the Beloved* (New York: Crossroads, 1992), 94–95.

16. Ronald Rolheiser, "Giving Our Deaths to Our Loved Ones" (November 11, 2001), http://www.ronrolheiser.com/columnarchive/?id=300.

17. Ronald Rolheiser, "There is a Season for Everything" (May 3, 2009), http://www.ronrolheiser.com/columnarchive/?id=459.

18. *The New York Times*, September 17, 2006.

19. Elisabeth Kübler-Ross, *Death: The Final Stage of Growth* (Englewood Cliffs, NJ: Prentice-Hall, 1975).

5. Grief, Ritual, and Growth

Opening quotation is from R. Scott Sullender, *Grief and Growth: Pastoral Resources for Emotional and Spiritual Growth* (New York/Mahwah, NJ: Paulist Press, 1985), 76.

1. Edna St. Vincent Millay, in a letter to Llewelyn Powys, April 20, 1931, http://www.berkshirelivingmag.com/Edna-St-Vincent-Millay-Steepletop-Linda-Ziskind-Julie-McCarthy-June-2010.

2. Dick Eggers, "Open Your Eyes," *The Word Among Us* (May 2008), 59.

3. Ibid., 60.

4. Sullender, *Grief and Growth*, 65–86. Another helpful resource is Alan D. Wolfelt, PhD, *Understanding Grief: Helping Yourself Heal* (Florence, KY: Accelerated Development, 1992).

5. Amy Plantinga Pauw, "Dying Well," in *Practicing Our Faith: A Way of Life for a Searching People*, ed. Dorothy C. Bass (San Francisco: Jossey-Bass Publisher, 1998), 163–77.

6. Pierre Benoit, "Resurrection: At the End of Time or Immediately After Death?" in *Immortality and Resurrection*, ed. Pierre Benoit and Roland Murphy, The New Concilium Series (New York: Herder and Herder, 1970), 114.

7. Kathleen Fischer, *Autumn Gospel* (New York/Mahwah, NJ: Paulist Press, 1995), 128.

8. Pauw, "Dying Well," 172–76.

9. Todd Van Beck, *Winning Ways* (Stamford, CT: Appleton & Lange, 1999).

10. General Introduction, no. 6, in the *Order of Christian Funerals* (Collegeville, MN: Liturgical Press, 1989).

11. Ibid., nos. 9, 11.

12. Nestor Gregoire, OMI, "Seven Essential Elements of a Healthy Funeral," *The Priest* (August 2004): 8–13. Used with permission.

13. Excerpt from the English translation of *Rite of Funerals* © 1970, International Commission on English in the Liturgy Corporation. All rights reserved. Used with permission.

6. Life After Death

1. Kent Nerburn, *Small Graces* (Novato, CA: New World Library, 1998), 50–53.

2. Anonymous, "A Parable." This unattributed story often appears online on blogs and parish Web sites. The version here comes from *Agape* 4:9 (September 1975): 19.

3. Ronald Rolheiser, "Second Birth" (July 3, 2005), http://www.ronrolheiser.com/columnarchive/?id=104.

4. Ronald Rolheiser, "Waiting for the Resurrection" (April 11, 2004), http://www.ronrolheiser.com/columnarchive/?id=176.

5. Raniero Cantalamessa, OFM Cap, "God Created Man for Life, Not Death," Gospel Commentary for the Feast of All Souls' Day (Rome, November 2, 2007), http://www.zenit.org/article-20893?l= English.

6. Kallistos Ware, *The Orthodox Way* (Crestwood, NY: St. Vladimir's Seminary Press, 1995), 98.

7. Ronald Rolheiser, "The Communion of Saints," *The Prairie Messenger* (November 5, 2006): 16.

8. Ronald Rolheiser, "The Benefits of Prayer for the Dead," *The Western Catholic Reporter* (November 4, 2001): 7.

7. Your Life Now

Opening quotation is from M. J. Ryan, in her praise for Dawna Markova's *I Will Not Die an Unlived Life* (Berkeley: Conari Press, 2000).

1. Megan McKenna, *Lent: Reflections and Stories on the Daily Readings* (Maryknoll, NY: Orbis, 1996), 168, 169.

2. Henri Nouwen, *Jesus: A Gospel* (Maryknoll, NY: Orbis, 2001), 77, 78.

3. Marjory Zoet Bankson, *Creative Aging* (Woodstock, VT: SkyLight Paths, 2010), 1–3.

4. Letter, Father Isaac Hecker to Mrs. King, August 2, 1864; archived at St. Paul's College in Washington, DC.

5. Phillip Bennett, *Let Yourself Be Loved* (New York/Mahwah, NJ: Paulist Press, 1997), 66. Used with permission.

8. Remember to Live!

Opening quotation is from J. Philip Newell, *Sounds of the Eternal: A Celtic Psalter* (Grand Rapids, MI: Wm. B. Eerdmans, 2002), 17.

1. Douglas Fisher, *I Have Given Them Your Word* (New York/Mahwah, NJ: Paulist Press, 1988), 156.

2. Mitch Albom, *Tuesdays with Morrie* (New York: Doubleday, 1997), 175, 176.

3. Melissa Musick Nussbaum, "My Mother's Keeper," *National Catholic Reporter* (July 10, 2009), 18.

4. Patricia Beattie Jung, "Differences Among the Elderly: Who is on the Road to Breman?" in *Growing Old in Christ*, ed. Stanley Hauerwas, Carole Bailey Stoneking, Keith G. Meador, and David Cloutier (Grand Rapids, MI: Wm. B. Eerdmans, 2003), 112–13.

5. Joan Chittister, *The Gift of Years* (New York: BlueBridge, 2008), 17–18.

6. Jacqueline McMakin and Rhoda Nary, The Doorway Series, 4 vols. (Washington, DC: Potter's House Book Service, 1993, 2004). The two organizations that helped train Jackie are the Church of the Saviour (www.inwardoutward.org/page/who-church-saviour/), an ecumenical network of churches in Washington, DC; and Lumunos (www.lumunos.org), a Christian organization that helps people connect their "call" with daily life.

7. Jacqueline McMakin, *Our Defining Moment: A Pocket Guide to Creating the Future We Truly Want.* For the widest distribution, Jackie has made a pdf of her book available for free at http://globalrenaissance.files.wordpress.com/2009/12/our-defining-moment.pdf.

8. George E. Vaillant, MD, *Aging Well* (New York: Little, Brown, 2002), 334–36.

9. Chittister, *The Gift of Years*, 199–200.

10. Ibid., 180–82.

11. Mark Davis Pickup, "Prepare for the Rejuvenating Gift of Retirement," *Western Catholic Reporter* (December 1, 2008): 10.

12. Enzo Bianchi, *Words of Spirituality* (Glasgow: Omnia Books, 2002), 34–36.

13. Ibid., 11–13; the quotation from Basil's Moral Rules is on 11.

14. Joan Chittister, *The Breath of the Soul: Reflections on Prayer* (New London, CT: Twenty-Third Publications, 2009), 63–64.

15. Ibid., 57–65.

16. Chittister, *The Gift of Years*, 97–99.

17. Albom, *Tuesdays with Morrie*, 175–76.

18. These two approaches appear separately in numerous places online. Neither one is attributed. Oftentimes the lists have been shortened or lengthened—for example, "*Ten* Things God Won't Ask You on Judgment Day," or "*Twenty* Things…"—and then the new version is reposted elsewhere, no doubt to be edited again by yet another reader.